4-

a taste of Tradition

a taste of Tradition

Pesach and Beyond

The Complete Guide
to Non-Gebrochs and
Kosher Gluten-Free Cooking

TAMAR ANSH

FELDHEIM PUBLISHERS
JERUSALEM   NEW YORK

ISBN 1-58330-788-5

FELDHEIM PUBLISHERS
POB 43163, Jerusalem, Israel

208 Airport Executive Park
Nanuet, NY 10954

www.feldheim.com

photography credits:
Sharon Bentov
Studio Sharon Bentov: Tel Aviv, Israel
Mobile: +972-54-4883570
Fax: +972-3-6493818
email: winckyst@netvision.net.il

Food and Prop stylist: Tamar Ansh
Layout and production editor: Frumet Buxbaum
Contributing proofreader: Frumet Buxbaum
Graphic artist: Michael Silverstein

Printed in Israel

In Appreciation

A cookbook of this nature incorporates many aspects and involves much more than just the author to see it to its completion. This has been many years in the dreaming stage, and quite a few months in the working stages...but without the help of all the individuals listed, no amount of dreaming would have ever gotten it off the ground!

I would first like to thank the special women who gave of their recipes to ensure that this cookbook would be top notch. Their contributions rounded out my collection and really added lots of "flavor" to an already rich compilation:

My mother, Mrs. Edith Shachter, for her numerous main dishes, mousse roll recipe, crinkle cookies, and eggplant ideas, just to name a few.

My mother-in-law, Mrs. Gloria Ansh, for permission to use several ideas from her cookbook, compiled with the sisterhood of Teaneck's JCC, entitled "Kosher Cuisine— A New Direction," a unique cookbook on its own, filled with over 200 pages of low fat and healthy kosher cooking ideas.

Mrs. Yides Buxbaum and Leah Buxbaum of Williamsburg, NY, for their excellent old world-style recipes and tips that add that really heimishe touch.

The list for the food committee is quite long; but each and every member in this committee was so devoted to its success that it is an honor to include each name. This committee includes our cooks for the photo shoots, the many friends and neighbors that donated special dishes and other items, the hours and hours of babysitting help, and our taste-testers. Most recipes have been tried and tested for years; those that were newer were taste-tested by the food committee and tweaked and corrected until they were taste-perfect:

F. Abramowitz, Reuven Ansh, Frumet Buxbaum, Bracha Fridrich, Devorah Harstein, Rachely Lever, Barbra Rock, Elisheva Rock, E. Schwalbe, and Chane Sepash. Mrs. T. Harkavey graciously gave of her time and expertise to create the beautiful flower-and-fruit arrangement featured in the fruit section of this cookbook.

It would be difficult to imagine this cookbook without the hard work of the photographer, Sharon Bentov. His beautiful photographs grace many of these pages; they are what make this cookbook a true work of art.

Last, but most certainly not least, I must extend a tremendous thank you to my dedicated friend, original layout artist, recipe editor, and all around touching-up person, Mrs. Frumet Buxbaum. The hours and hours she spent on editing each recipe and retouching photos and on each page's layout, went far and beyond the call of duty. It is her work above all else that has created the clear and spectacular cookbook you now hold in your hands.

It has been an honor and a pleasure to work with the special staff at Feldheim Publishers. I would like to thank R' Mendy Feldheim for his encouragement and dedicated attention to this project, Deena Nataf for her final proofreading, and Michael Silverstein for all the rest.

Far too often, people have the impression that on Pesach, there is "nothing to eat" the whole time – all the more so when, on top of all the other Pesach food restrictions, they also don't use matzo meal. This cookbook is coming to change this attitude, to show that Pesach, even when one does not "broch" (i.e., does not use matzo flour of any kind), can be beautiful, delicious, and have plenty of variety to last much more than just eight days. It can even be relatively easy to do!

Furthermore, there are so many people today who have a serious dietary need for gluten-free recipes. This new, all kosher gluten-free cookbook will make a lasting and tasteful impression all year long for anyone who wants to cook wheat- and-gluten-free.

It is my heartfelt wish that this cookbook will open new avenues for you, the reader, and for you, the cook, in Pesach non-gebrochs food preparation, and in kosher gluten-free cooking. Pesach especially is supposed to be our time of freedom, our time of malchus, a time for our nation to relax and enjoy a feeling of royalty; and I would like to see it become so, once again.

I close with a prayer that this book will enhance the simchas Yom Tov of Klal Yisroel, and thereby give nachas to the Borei Olam, Who, much more than I can write here, is really the One Who helped me organize and create this special book.

טוֹב לְהֹדוֹת לַה'
וּלְזַמֵּר לְשִׁמְךָ עֶלְיוֹן

Tamar Ansh
I Adar 5765
Jerusalem

H ELPFUL   T IPS
(before, during, and after Pesach)

✦ Prepare pre-Pesach meals well in advance for the family so that there will be several days worth of good, healthy meals during those last, hectic days before Yom Tov. You will save money because you won't have to buy take-out foods, and you will also have more stamina for Yom Tov preparations. It will be relaxing to know that there is something ready to serve immediately. When preparing these meals, use disposable containers, paper plates, and plastic utensils. Stock up on them a few weeks in advance to prevent running out at the last minute. Some of the meals prepared should be chometz-free, so the last two or three days the children won't be running around the house with chometzdik hands and faces.

✦ When buying fresh fruits and vegetables, keep in mind that this week's purchases will probably be the largest order of the year. Consult with the lists from the previous year (see last tip below) concerning the quantities used in the past. It might be necessary to buy over 20 lbs. (about 10 kilo) of onions and potatoes alone. This is a very normal amount even if it is the first Pesach you are making.

✦ At the end of every Pesach, while packing away your dishes, secure them closed in either sealed boxes or plastic garbage bags. This will prevent them from becoming dusty, thereby saving time of having to rinse each item the next year.

✦ At the end of every Pesach, write down how much was ordered, and how much as used, of all food items. This makes a huge difference especially with fresh produce and meats, since by the next year you won't remember so easily what and how much was ordered from the year before. In addition, it is also helpful to mark down how many people consumed the food. Any non-perishable items that were stored away for the next Pesach should be noted so that when shopping again, those items do not have to be bought, i.e., shelving paper, oil, dish soap, etc. Remember to leave these lists somewhere handy and easy to remember, so you won't have to scrounge around for them at the last minute.

H E L P F U L H I N T S
(for utilizing this cookbook)

✦ *For people who have the chumrah to use only peeled vegetables, Peppers can be peeled with a normal carrot peeler and a small dollop of patience. Tomatoes and peaches can be peeled very easily by first placing them in a bowl with very hot, boiled water for a few minutes, though not too long, then pulling them out with a fork and peeling with your fingers under cold running water. One bowl should be designated for this purpose only, and label it as the"peeling bowl" since the water is very hot and the reason people do not use the peels is because of a doubt of chometz on the outside of them.*

✦ *Food processors are mentioned quite often in this cookbook. Many recipes can be made without one, but it will help tremendously to buy at least an inexpensive one that grinds, grates, and mixes. A hand mixer (especially one that comes with a stand) is also very helpful.*

✦ *"T." stands for tablespoon; "tsp." stands for teaspoon*

✦ *1 lemon = 2–3 T. fresh juice*

✦ *Boiled potatoes that have cooled down can be mashed up much easier and fluffier, if one raw egg, or 1–2 egg whites are added to them when mashing. The best time to mash potatoes is while they are still hot, using a small amount of the hot water they were boiled in.*

✦ *Raw meats cut much easier if they are still partially frozen.*

✦ *Many Ashkenazim have the custom not to use garlic on Pesach. For those who follow this custom, simply delete it from the recipe when cooking.*

✦ *To get more juice out of oranges and lemons let them stand at room temperature and then roll them firmly against the counter for a few seconds before squeezing.*

✦ *Read through the entire recipe and instructions from beginning to end before beginning and prepare ingredients in advance.*

✦ *Oven temperatures mentioned in this cookbook were rounded off for the convenience of the reader. In all cases, the slight difference does not affect the way the recipe cooks (e.g. 350°F is literally 176.66°C, and was rounded to 180°C).*

Happy Cooking!

Table Of Contents

Salads & Dressings

Cabbage Apple Salad

Serves 6

2 cups shredded green cabbage
2 green apples, cubed
3 red apples, cubed
1 20 oz. can pineapple tidbits with
   juice

1 T. lemon juice
4 T. mayonnaise
1/2 cup Craisins
1/2 cup black raisins, optional
1/2 cup cashew nuts

Note:
Recipe for
homemade Pesach
mayonnaise can
be found on
page 12.

Mix all the ingredients together in large bowl, except for cashews.
Refrigerate. Right before serving, toss salad and add cashews.

Fresh Spinach Salad

Serves 6

1 large head spinach
2 firm red tomatoes, cubed, or 20
cherry tomatoes
2 cucumbers, peeled and sliced
1 small red onion, sliced, optional
1 large carrot, shredded
1/2 cup sliced or slivered almonds

Dressing:
4 T. freshly squeezed lemon juice
1/2 tsp. salt
1/4 tsp. pepper
1/2 tsp. garlic powder, optional
3 T. salad oil

Prepare this recipe right before serving. Wash each of the spinach
leaves very well so they won't have sand on them. Dry the leaves
carefully. In a large bowl, layer the spinach leaves, then the rest of
the vegetables carefully on top. Place the ingredients for dressing in
another bowl, mix vigorously and pour over all. Toss salad to coat
evenly. Sprinkle nuts over top and serve.

Instant Pickle Slices

Serves 8

Note:
This recipe
works best if the
cucumbers are
 left unpeeled.

10 cucumbers, washed and sliced
1 cup (wine) vinegar
3 cups water
2 T. salt
4 tsp. sugar

1 small sliced onion
3–4 garlic cloves
3 black peppercorns
2–3 whole cloves, optional

Mix all ingredients except cucumber slices into a pot and stir for a minute. Add cucumbers. Bring to a boil on stovetop, then let simmer for 5 minutes or so until color changes to light green. Turn off flame. Add peppercorns and cloves. Cool and refrigerate.

Stewed Red Cabbage Salad

Serves 4–6

1 medium head red cabbage, shredded
2 large onions, chopped
2 large green apples, peeled
*   and chopped*

2 T. oil
3/4 cup raisins
1 T. brown or white sugar
1–2 T. lemon juice

Put cabbage in a pot, cover with water and bring to a boil. Remove from heat and drain. Cabbage will be blue. Saute onions and apples in oil for 5 to 10 minutes. Turn off flame. Add in raisins, cabbage, sugar, and lemon juice. Mix well. Cabbage will return to its original color. Cover pot and simmer on low heat for 30 minutes. Serve hot or cold.

Kohlrabi Salad

Serves 4

3 Kohlrabi, sliced into strips
1 tsp. salt

1/2 tsp. pepper
1 T. oil

Steam kohlrabi strips in covered saucepan for about 10 minutes. Turn off flame. Keep covered for an additional 5 minutes. Drain and season with remaining ingredients. Refrigerate before serving.

Marinated Fresh Vegetables   *Serves 6*

Use any combination of: carrot slices, zucchini slices, sliced peppers, cauliflower or broccoli florets, celery chunks, mushrooms, and cherry tomatoes.

Marinade:
1 cup olive oil
1/2 cup (wine) vinegar
1/2 cup water
1 T. sugar

1 tsp. each of thyme, marjoram
*   and basil*
dash of pepper
1 large garlic clove, minced
1 large bay leaf

Combine ingredients for the marinade in a food processor or blender. Place the vegetables of your choice in a container and pour the marinade over them. Store in the refrigerator overnight. Before serving, remove the bay leaf and drain vegetables completely.

Cabbage Medley   *Serves 6–8*

1 large head green cabbage
1 large head purple cabbage
4 large carrots
1/2 small green pepper, optional
1/2 tsp. pepper

1/2 cup sugar
3/4 cup (wine) vinegar
1 3/4 cups water
3 T. mayonnaise
2 T. coarse salt

Shred all the vegetables into a very big bowl. Sprinkle the coarse salt over the vegetables and toss. Add the rest of the ingredients aside from the mayonnaise into the vegetables and let it stand for five minutes. Then transfer it to a different container, leaving most of the liquid behind. Add the mayonnaise, toss and refrigerate overnight. This keeps well for close to a week.

Tip:
You may find that for cabbage, the slicer blade on the food processor works better than the grater blade. The salad makes a tremendous amount, so use a big bowl. It shrinks considerably after you add the rest of ingredients.

Trifle Salad

Serves 8–10

Tip:
Shredding the
lettuce by hand
keeps it fresher
longer.

Note:
Two delicious
dressings recom-
mended for this tri-
fle are "All Natural
Salad Dressing"
and "Lemon Salad
Dressing" found on
page 13.

1 head lettuce, washed and shredded
5 medium cucumbers, cubed
2–3 cups cherry tomatoes
1 white or red onion, sliced into rings
1 each of red, yellow, and green
pepper, sliced in thin rings
2 medium carrots, shredded

2 cups purple cabbage, shredded
4 medium zucchini, shredded
1 can mandarin oranges, optional
1 cup sliced or slivered almonds
alfalfa sprouts
Craisins
1 pineapple ring

Place shredded cabbage and lettuce into a trifle bowl. Continue layering each vegetable in a colorful order, except for the peppers.
Place the pepper rings in a decorative pattern on top. Top the trifle
with the pineapple ring in the middle with Craisins around it, and
a cherry tomato or more Craisins in its center. Then arrange several mandarin orange slices outside of the ring and alfalfa sprouts
around the outer edge. Sprinkle almonds over the top. Serve
immediately with a choice of dressings on the side.

Lettuce Salad

Serves 6

1/2 cup sugar
1/2 cup (wine) vinegar
1/2 cup oil
1 tsp. paprika

2 T. ground or slivered almonds
1 large iceberg or romaine lettuce
2 cups radicchio lettuce combo
1/2 small red onion

Mix together sugar, vinegar, oil and paprika in jar. Let stand in
refrigerator. Right before serving, cut up lettuce and place in salad
bowl. Add onion rings. Sprinkle almonds over top of salad. Pour
dressing over salad and serve.

Zucchini Salad

Serves 4

3 medium zucchini, washed or peeled,
*   sliced thinly*
1 small onion, diced
1/2 red pepper, sliced in strips

1/2 cup (wine) vinegar
1 1/2 tsp. salt
1/2 cup water
1/8 tsp. pepper

Combine all into a bowl, mix and refrigerate overnight.

Carrot Salad

Serves 8

8 large carrots, peeled and shredded
2 apples, peeled and chopped
1/2 cup white or black raisins,
optional

1 cup pineapple pieces
1/2 cup sugar
1 tsp. cinnamon
2 T. lemon juice

Place shredded carrots and apples in a bowl. Add the lemon juice right away and toss together to prevent apples from turning brown. Add raisins, pineapples, sugar and cinnamon. Refrigerate for a few hours. Taste for sweetness.

Coleslaw

Serves 6–8

1 head green cabbage
4–5 large carrots
3/4 T. salt
1/2 cup (wine) vinegar

2/3 cup sugar
1/2 tsp. pepper
4 T. mayonnaise

Shred vegetables and place in a large bowl. Sprinkle salt over them, then add vinegar, sugar, and pepper. Mix well and then add mayonnaise. Place in covered container and let stand overnight in refrigerator.

Mushroom Marinade

Serves 4

Note:
Use fresh mushrooms either raw or steamed whole for several minutes.

1 medium can whole mushrooms or
    one box fresh mushrooms
1 T. lemon juice
2 T. (wine) vinegar
3 T. oil
1/2 tsp. salt

1/4 tsp. pepper
1/4 tsp. sugar
1/2 tsp. dill
1/2 tsp. parsley
1/2 small onion, diced
1 each of red and green pepper, diced

Pour lemon juice, vinegar and oil into a bowl. Add spices, sugar, dill, and parsley. Mix well. Then add in mushrooms, onion, and peppers. Mix well and allow to marinate in refrigerator for several hours or overnight.

Nutty Cabbage Salad

Serves 4–6

2–3 cups shredded purple cabbage
1–2 cups shredded green cabbage
1/2 cup slivered almonds
1/2 cup coarsely chopped walnuts
    or pecans

Dressing:
1/2 cup oil
2 T. (wine) vinegar
1 tsp. salt
2 tsp. sugar

Brown all the nuts for 2–3 minutes in a dry skillet, until light brown. Toss cabbage in a large bowl together with browned nuts. Mix the marinade ingredients and pour over salad. Refrigerate several hours before serving.

Cucumber and Carrot Salad

Serves 4

1 large cucumber or 3 small ones,
    scrubbed well or peeled
2 medium carrots
2 finely chopped scallions

1/2 cup finely chopped fresh parsley
1 T. sugar
3 T. (wine) vinegar
salt and pepper to taste

Cut cucumber into cubes, to make about 3 cups. Place in bowl. Shred carrots and add to bowl. Add everything else and toss well to blend. Serve chilled.

Spinach Dip

2 1/2 cups frozen or fresh spinach
1 cup mayonnaise
1/2 cup chopped green pepper
1/2 cup chopped onion

small bunch fresh parsley
    or 1 T. dried
1 tsp. salt
1/4 tsp. pepper

Tip:
Saute the onion until light brown before adding for a less sharp taste.

Dairy Variation:
Substitute 1/2 cup each of cream cheese and plain yogurt in place of mayonnaise.

Blend all the ingredients in food processor. Place in container and refrigerate.

Cucumber Mold

Serves 6–8

2 packages lemon-flavored gelatin
2 cups boiling water
1/3 cup (wine) vinegar
1/2 tsp. salt, optional
2 medium cucumbers, peeled,
shredded and drained

1/2 cup celery, finely chopped
1–2 T. white horseradish, grated
1 T. grated onion
1/2 T. chopped dill
1 medium cucumber, cut into
20 thin slices

Dissolve the gelatin in water. Stir in vinegar. Let cool, stirring occasionally until it has the consistency of unbeaten egg whites. Fold in the remaining ingredients, except the sliced cucumber. Rinse the jello ring/mold with cold water. Do not dry. Line bottom of mold with cucumber slices, pour in the gelatin mixture and let set.

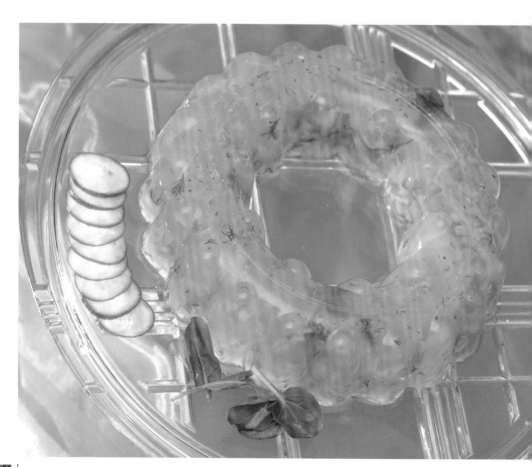

Beet Salad

Serves 6

5 medium-large beets, peeled and
    quartered (check for worms)
1 small onion, sliced thin
1/4 cup sugar

2 T. lemon juice or (wine) vinegar
1/4 tsp. salt
1/4 tsp. pepper, optional

Place the beets in a pot and cover with water. Boil them for about
45 minutes or until they are soft. Cool overnight in the refrigerator
together with some of the water they were boiled in, as they will
grate easier when cold. Grate the beets into a bowl and add the
rest of the ingredients. Serve cold.

Tip:
For those of you who like to do things ahead of time, the beets can be boiled in large quantities, grated, and frozen just so. Then when you are ready to use them, you can just pull them out of the freezer, defrost them, and you're all set to make your salads and chrain in one day.

Waldorf Salad

Serves 4

5–6 large apples, Macintosh or
    Granny Smith
2 fat stalks celery, diced
10 walnut halves, coarsely chopped
2 T. sugar

1/8 tsp. salt
1 tsp. lemon juice
1/8 tsp. cinnamon
1/2 cup dark raisins, optional
1 T. mayonnaise

Grate the apples into a bowl. Sprinkle in the lemon juice and stir.
Add in the celery together with the coarsely chopped walnuts. Put
in the rest of the other ingredients and mix. Refrigerate before
serving.

Tip:
The lemon juice prevents the apples from turning brown.

Cucumber and Tomato Salad

Serves 4

3 medium cucumbers, peeled
3 firm, red tomatoes, washed well
1/2 cup red or white onion, chopped
2 T. fresh dill, chopped,
    or 1/2 tsp. dried

4 T. olive oil
1/2 tsp. ground cumin
2 T. (wine) vinegar
1/2 tsp. salt
1/4 tsp. pepper

Chop cucumbers and tomatoes into cubes. Place the rest of the
ingredients in a bowl and stir briskly. Add cucumbers and tomatoes. Toss well and serve immediately.

Colorful Salad Supreme   *Serves 6–8*

1 medium onion, sliced
2 zucchini, scrubbed but not peeled
2 carrots
1 green pepper
1 red pepper
2 stalks celery
3 cups broccoli spears
2 cups cauliflower

Marinade:
3/4 cups cider vinegar (preferred),
    or wine vinegar
1/2 cup (olive) oil
2 T. sugar
1/2 tsp. oregano
1/4 tsp. pepper

Place sliced onion on the bottom of a pot. Slice zucchini and carrots into thin rounds and layer on top of onion. Slice peppers into thin strips and add. Then cut celery into small chunks and add. Steam together with about 3–4 T. of water for about 5 minutes. Add broccoli and cauliflower and steam for another 8 minutes. Turn off flame, leave pot covered and let cool down for 15 minutes. Remove from pot with slotted spoon and place in large plastic bowl or container. Mix the ingredients for marinade together, and pour over vegetables. Refrigerate for several hours or overnight. Serve cold.

Cucumber Salad   *Serves 6–8*

15–20 medium cucumbers,
    peeled and sliced
1 small onion, sliced thinly
1 T. coarse or regular salt

4 T. sugar
3/4 cup (wine) vinegar
1/2 tsp. paprika
1/2 tsp. pepper

Place cucumber slices into bowl, sprinkle salt over them and mix together. Let stand in bowl for 1/2 hour. Squeeze out water by hand from cucumbers and transfer them to another bowl or container. Rinse off slightly to remove excess salt. Add the onion, sugar, and vinegar. Mix and add remaining ingredients. Refrigerate several hours or overnight.

Avocado Guacamole

Serves 4–6

4 ripe avocados, cubed
1 large onion, diced
3 garlic cloves, diced

1/4 cup olive oil
1 tsp. salt
1/2 tsp. pepper
2 tsp. fresh lemon juice

Variation:
Puree everything, adding in several fresh sprigs parsley. Serve with vegetables. To keep it green until serving, add the pit of the avocado to the center of the mixture. Remove before serving.

Saute onions and garlic in olive oil until lightly brown. Place avocados into a small bowl. Pour lemon juice and seasonings over it. Add onion and garlic mixture and mix. Refrigerate until serving.

Mayonnaise

Yields 2–2 1/2 cups

2 whole raw eggs
1 tsp. salt
dash pepper
2 T. (wine) vinegar

2 T. lemon juice
3 T. sugar
2 cups oil (not olive oil)

Whip eggs in food processor with whipping blade for 2 minutes on medium/high speed. While processor is still on, add everything else except for oil. Then add oil very slowly. Let it keep blending for another 10–15 minutes until very firm. Refrigerate overnight. Keeps well in refrigerator for about 2 weeks.

Tip:
Blending this in a food processor will keep the ingredients from separating.

Oil and Vinegar Dressing

1 cup salad oil
3/4 cup (wine) vinegar
1 tsp. salt
1/2 tsp. pepper
1/2 tsp. oregano

1/2 tsp. basil
1 tsp. onion powder
1 tsp. garlic powder
1 bay leaf
1/2 tsp. marjoram, optional

Mix all ingredients and shake vigorously. Pour over any fresh salad. Best if made a day or two in advance.

Tomato Salad Dressing

5 fully ripe tomatoes, diced
1/4 cup oil
2 T. (wine) vinegar
2 T. sliced scallion
2 tsp. salt

1/4 tsp. paprika
1/8 tsp. pepper
3/4 tsp. crushed marjoram leaves,
    optional

Puree all the ingredients in food processor until smooth, about 10 seconds. Open the processor and scrape down the sides; repeat pureeing. Cover and refrigerate until serving. Excellent over salad greens.

All Natural Salad Dressing

1/2 small onion, optional
2 scallions
1 small garlic clove
1 green pepper
1 red pepper
4 ripe tomatoes, peeled
1 stalk celery, optional
3 big sprigs fresh parsley, or 1 T. dried

3 big sprigs fresh dill, or 1 tsp. dried
1–2 tsp. salt
1/2 tsp. pepper
2 tsp. sugar
2 T. (wine) vinegar
1 T. freshly squeezed lemon juice
2 cups mayonnaise

Note:
This dressing keeps well in the fridge for about two weeks.

In a food processor, puree all vegetables until liquid-like consistency, doing half at a time if necessary. In the last batch add the remaining ingredients and puree well. Let stand in a covered container overnight in the refrigerator. Serve over fresh salads.

Russian Dressing

1 cup mayonnaise
1/2 cup Pesachdik ketchup
1 T. onion powder

1 T. garlic powder
1 tsp. paprika
1 T. lemon juice or vinegar

Mix all ingredients well until smooth.

Lemon Salad Dressing

2 cups mayonnaise
1/2 cup lemon juice
1 tsp. onion powder
1 tsp. garlic powder

1 tsp. paprika
1/2 tsp. pepper
6–8 sprigs fresh dill or 1 tsp. dried

Mix together well until there are no lumps and it has a liquid-like consistency. Can be used as a dressing over salad or as a dip with cut-up vegetables.

N O T E S   T O   R E M E M B E R

Soups & Then Some

Heimishe Chicken Soup, page 16
Non-Gebrochs Kneidlach, page 25

Heimishe Chicken Soup *Serves 10–12*

Tips:
A good idea for conserving on the chickens is to save all the necks and wings of the chickens you are cooking for your seudos and use those in the soup.

The longer a soup cooks the more flavor it has and the saltier it becomes. If soup is too salty, add 2 medium potatoes, peeled and cut into chunks, to absorb salt.

See pages 24 and 25 for soup accompaniments.

chicken parts, turkey necks
    or bones of both
2 medium-large onions, chopped
5 garlic cloves, minced
3 large carrots, cut into chunks
3 zucchini, cut into chunks
1 large leek, chopped
1 celery head, halved
2 stalks celery, chopped

1 parsley root, peeled, optional
1 ripe red tomato, halved
1 1/2 T. salt
3/4 tsp. pepper
bunch fresh dill, or 1/2 T. dried
bunch fresh parsley, or 1/2 T. dried
small amount of oil
chunk of pumpkin, chopped,
    optional

Place onions and garlic in bottom of a 10–15 quart pot and saute in about 2 T. of oil until clear. Add in chicken and/or turkey parts. Then add in the vegetables. Sprinkle in seasonings and fill pot with water to cover. Put this up early in the morning and once it starts to boil, turn down to a low flame and let it cook 4–5 hours or even all day. Taste for salt adjustments.

For the seder night, all the extra vegetables are a great side dish as they are easy to digest, and a nice accompaniment to the main course you will be serving. This is usually all you will really need for the Seder meal, because most people are pretty full from everything that was already consumed before the actual meal began.

Heimishe Borscht

Serves 10–12

10 large beets, quartered
2 1/2 quarts water
3 meat bones and/or 1–2 pieces flanken
1/4 cup lemon juice

1/2–3/4 cup sugar
2 1/2 tsp salt
5 eggs
4 potatoes

Put the potatoes up to cook until soft. Reserve on the side in a separate container. Place the remaining ingredients except the eggs into an 8 quart pot, and bring to a boil. Lower flame and cook gently for 1 1/2 hours. Remove the beets and meat bones from pot. In a large bowl, beat the eggs very well. Slowly pour 1 cup of beet liquid into egg mixture, beating vigorously while pouring to prevent curdling. It should be a nice pink color. Pour mixture into remaining borscht and mix thoroughly. Slice the reserved potatoes and serve together with the hot soup.

Zucchini Squash Soup

Serves 8

6–8 medium zucchini, chopped
5 onions, chopped
1/4 cup oil
1 1/2 tsp. curry

2–3 tsp. salt
1/8 tsp. cayenne pepper
("paprika charifa")
4 cups chicken broth

Saute onions and zucchini in oil until soft, for about 1 to 1 1/2 hours. Add in seasonings. Puree vegetables until smooth. Return to pot and add chicken broth. Simmer for another 1/2 hour.

Tip:
For many soups found in this chapter, your leftover chicken soup can be used as the broth called for in the recipes. Keep in mind the soup will then be fleishig.

Onion Soup

Serves 6–8

5 large onions, diced
1/4 cup oil or butter
2 T. potato starch and
4 T. cold water

11 cups water
2 tsp. salt
1 tsp. sugar
1/2 tsp. pepper

1/2 cup dry or semi-dry
white wine
3 T. onion soup mix

Variation:
For a dairy soup, add a small handful of grated parmesan, mozzarella, or yellow cheese to each portion before serving.

Saute onions in oil or butter for 15–20 minutes. Add seasonings. Dissolve potato starch with 4 T. cold water. Add to pot and stir immediately. Add liquid ingredients and simmer for 2 hours.

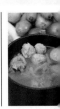

Basic Beet Borscht

Serves 8–10

Tip:
For a thicker and lighter soup, whip up 2 eggs in a separate bowl, then add a small amount of the warm soup to them, mixing quickly and thoroughly. Return to soup in pot. Stir but do not reboil.

*8–10 large beets, peeled, washed well,
    and cut into chunks*
2 tsp. salt
3 large garlic cloves

juice of one lemon
3–4 T. sugar, optional
water to cover

Place beets in a large pot and fill until the top with water, making sure beets are well covered. Place lid on pot and boil until tender, at least an hour. Poke with a fork to ensure that they are soft. Keep covered after boiling so they will stay soft until grated. Add garlic cloves to the hot water. Remove beet pieces from pot and grate coarsely, reserving the juice they were boiled in. Put the beets back into the pot, together with rest of ingredients. Boil again for another 1/2 hour. Place in jars or containers in fridge and serve cold. Keeps well all week long.

Hearty Vegetable Soup

Serves 10

2 large onions, sliced
5 garlic cloves, diced
2–3 stalks celery, diced
2 zucchini, cut into chunks
2–3 carrots, cut into rounds
1–2 small potatoes, cut into chunks
1 green pepper, diced
1 red pepper, diced
large piece of pumpkin, chunked
1 celery head, peeled and halved
or quartered

1 parsley root, peeled and cut into
    chunks
1 box fresh mushrooms, cleaned and
    sliced
1 bunch fresh parsley or 1/2 T. dried
1 bunch fresh dill or 1 tsp. dried
2–3 tsp. salt
3/4 tsp. pepper
1 T. onion powder
4 T. tomato sauce or 1 fresh tomato,
    diced
2 T. olive oil

Place onions and garlic in bottom of a 10–12 quart pot and saute
in the oil until clear. Add water until pot is halfway full. Then put
in all the other vegetables. Add seasonings. Then add in tomato
sauce and stir. Heat until boiling point, then reduce flame and continue to cook for at least three hours. The longer you cook it, the
better it will taste.

For a thicker soup, puree for about 1–2 minutes with an immersion blender directly in the pot after it has cooked about 2 hours.
This method also opens up the flavor of the vegetables more and
increases its aesthetic appeal. The soup freezes well.

Meat 'n Cabbage Soup

Serves 4–6

2 lbs. flanken, cut into chunks
1 large onion, sliced
2 garlic cloves, diced
1 large head green or
    purple cabbage, shredded
1/4 cup freshly squeezed lemon juice

1 small green pepper, diced
1 stalk celery, diced, optional
6 red tomatoes, peeled and cubed
2 tsp. brown sugar *
2 tsp. salt
1/2 tsp. pepper

Brown meat for 15 minutes, together with onion and garlic. Cover
with water completely and cook for 2 hours. Add everything else
and continue cooking for another 2 hours.

*Suggestion:
For those who do
not use brown sugar
on Pesach: Brown 2
T. white sugar in a
separate pot over a
small flame and stir
constantly. When it
turns light brown,
remove from fire
immediately and
add to the boiling
soup.

Dairy Variation:
Substitute milk for
pareve milk and
sprinkle some
grated cheese on
top of florets before
serving.

Garden Broccoli Soup

Serves 4

1 large head fresh broccoli or
   1 bag Bodek frozen
1 large onion, diced
3 scallions, diced
3 T. butter or olive oil
1 green pepper, diced
1 red pepper, diced

1 potato, peeled and chopped
6 cups water
1 cup pareve milk, optional
1/2 tsp. pepper
2 1/2 tsp. salt
1/2 tsp. dried parsley
10 broccoli florets, reserved

Saute onion and peppers in oil until golden brown. Add in scallions, potato, broccoli and seasonings. Cover with water and
bring to a boil, then simmer for 35 minutes until soft. Puree in
blender for a minute to make it thick and chunky, or completely
puree for smoother texture. For a creamier consistency, add
pareve milk. Serve hot with reserved florets to garnish.

Thick Yellow Vegetable Soup

Serves 8–10

1–2 medium onions, sliced
1 green pepper, chopped
1 red pepper, chopped
2 orange or yellow peppers, chopped
2 medium sweet potatoes, cubed
2 medium potatoes, cubed
1 butternut squash, chunked
5–7 large carrots, sliced

large piece of pumpkin, chunked,
    optional
3 ripe tomatoes, chopped
2–3 tsp. salt
1/2 tsp. pepper
small bunch each
    fresh dill and parsley
2 T. olive oil

In a 7–8 quart (or larger) pot, saute onions and peppers in the olive oil. Add in the spices and all other vegetables. Fill with water until almost the top of the pot. Bring to a boil and then simmer for about 2 hours on a low flame until completely soft. Puree until smooth. Freezes well.

Gluten-Free Minestrone Soup

Serves 6–8

1 onion, diced finely
1 each green, red, and orange peppers,
    diced
1/2 head red cabbage, sliced
3 carrots, sliced thin
large chunk of pumpkin (about
    1 lb./ 400 gram size), chunked
1 small sweet potato
1 1/2–2 cups frozen spinach
2 overripe tomatoes, diced

1 cup tomato sauce or paste
2 T. olive or canola oil
1/2 T. salt
1/2 tsp. pepper
1 tsp. oregano
1/2 tsp. basil
small bunch fresh parsley
8–9 cups water
1/2 cup any shaped small Gefen
    Gluten-Free Noodles, optional

Layer onions and peppers in the bottom of the pan with oil. Start to saute while layering in the cabbage and tomato sauce. Layer in all the rest of the vegetables together with all the seasonings. **Do not add noodles yet**. Cover with water and heat until it boils, then simmer for 2 hours.

Place an immersion blender into the soup and puree for only a few seconds; this will add flavor and richness to the soup. Add the Gluten-Free Noodles. Let it simmer another 5–7 minutes and serve immediately.

Mushroom Soup

Serves 6

1/2 cup margarine or olive oil
one onion, diced
4 stalks celery, diced
4–5 T. potato starch
1/4 cup cold water

6 cups chicken soup broth
1 tsp. salt
1/2 tsp. pepper
1 lb./1/2 kilo fresh mushrooms

Saute onion in oil or margarine until soft. Add celery and saute 10 more minutes. In a separate bowl, mix together the cold water and potato starch until smooth. Add this to the sauteing vegetables and stir immediately to keep it from becoming lumpy. Add the 6 cups of broth slowly, 1–2 cups at a time while continuously stirring. Add the fresh mushrooms and seasonings. Simmer for another 20–25 minutes. Turn off heat and puree until smooth. Serve with garnish of fresh parsley sprig in the center of each bowl.

Carrot Soup

Serves 4

6 large carrots, sliced into thin rounds
1 large onion, diced
1 green pepper, diced
2 stalks celery, diced
6 T. olive oil
4 medium, red and firm tomatoes,
    cubed

3 cups chicken soup broth
2 tsp. salt
3/4 tsp. pepper
chopped fresh parsley

Saute onions, carrots, celery, and pepper in oil for 15 minutes. Add in cubed tomatoes and saute another 2–4 minutes. Add the water and seasonings and cook together for an hour. Puree halfway in blender so that the soup has a thicker, but still somewhat chunky consistency. Garnish with fresh parsley in each bowl.

Leek Soup

Serves 4–6

1/2 cup olive oil or margarine
3 leeks, cleaned, thoroughly checked,
    and sliced
1 medium onion, diced
4 medium potatoes, cubed
1/2 tsp. dried tarragon

1/2 tsp. thyme
4 cups vegetable or chicken broth,
    or water
1 tsp. salt

Saute the leeks and onion in oil for 10 minutes. Add the water or broth and seasonings. If you used only water, you may have to add more salt. Add potatoes and simmer for 1 1/2 hours. Puree until smooth. Serve warm. If soup is too thick, add more liquid before turning off the flame.

Asparagus Soup

Serves 6–8

1–1 1/2 lbs./500–650 grams fresh or
    frozen asparagus
2 T. olive oil
2 large onions
2 small potatoes, peeled and cubed
1 medium carrot
1 red tomato, optional
2 tsp. salt

1/2 tsp. pepper
1 bay leaf
small sprig fresh parsley,
    plus more for garnishing
1/2 tsp. marjoram
1/2 tsp. cumin
1 tsp. paprika
6 cups water

Saute onions in olive oil until browned. Add in potatoes and only two cups water. Simmer for 15 minutes. Add in all other ingredients and cook for 1 1/2–2 hours. Turn off flame. Remove bay leaf. Puree soup until partly smooth and partly chunky. Can be served either warm or cold with reserved parsley sprig in center of each bowl.

Cucumber Soup

Serves 6

Dairy Variation:
After pureeing,
and in 1 cup of sour
cream and blend
well.

2 onions, diced

2 T. olive oil

3 potatoes, peeled and cubed

3 cups water

2 tsp. salt

1/2 tsp. pepper

small bunch each
  fresh dill and parsley

5 medium cucumbers,
  peeled and cubed

1 leek, washed, thoroughly checked,
  and chopped

Saute the onions and leek in olive oil for 10 minutes. Add water,
potatoes, dill, parsley, and seasonings. Cover pot and cook for an
hour, until potatoes are soft. Add cucumbers and cook another 3
minutes. Remove from heat and puree until mostly smooth. Serve
warm or cold, with an additional small sprig of fresh parsley in
each bowl to garnish.

Soup Accompaniments

*Tip:
The lokshen will
fry up much
thinner if you
first place the mix-
ture in the fridge.

Lokshen

Serves 8–10

4 eggs

1/4 cup potato starch

1/3 cup water

Beat all of the ingredients together until as smooth as possible.
Place in refrigerator for a few hours.* Remove bubbles from the
top of the mixture before frying up. Heat some oil in a frying pan,
or use a non-stick pan. When oil is hot, pour in some batter, and
rotating the pan, spread the batter evenly around the bottom of it.
Fry for about a minute. As the blintze begins to curl, flip out onto
a plate. Continue with remaining batter. When you are finished,
roll up the pile of egg blintzes and cut into thin strips. Serve in hot
soup.

Non-Gebrochs Kneidlach

Yields 15–20 balls

Note:
Kneidlach can be
made in advance
and frozen. Remove
from freezer and
place in soup
approximately
45 minutes before
soup finishes
cooking.

1 lb./1/2 kilo ground white chicken or
white turkey
2 whole raw eggs
1/2 tsp. salt

1 potato, cooked and mashed
1 small onion, diced or pureed

Combine all the above ingredients and mix well. Refrigerate for
about an hour or so to make the batter firm. Make small balls out
of it and drop into boiling hot water. Cook for about 3/4 of an
hour. Add to soup pot about 45 minutes before soup finishes
cooking.

"Hubbub"

Ratio for this recipe is 1 T. potato starch per 1 egg.

Whip up the whites of egg(s) alone. Whip yolks with spices such as
pepper, paprika, onion powder, and garlic powder, to taste. Then
add the starch measured per egg to the yolks and beat until blended well. Fold the whites into the yolks. Pour the whole mixture
into a pot of rapidly boiling water and let it simmer for 15 minutes.
Remove from pot, drain. Separate into as many pieces as you like
and put some into each person's soup when serving.

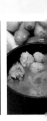

NOTES TO REMEMBER

Fish

Roasted Garlic Fish, page 36

◆ When ordering fresh fish, clean it and make it, or freeze it right away. If you leave it in your refrigerator more than a day it will not be fresh tasting anymore, and it will start to "go off".

◆ Clean off scales by holding the fish under cold water and scraping with a sharp, non-serrated knife, firmly against the direction of the scales.

◆ Always remove the guts of fish pieces before using, as they make the fish bitter tasting.

◆ Baked fish cooks best on a high temperature for less time.

◆ Done in fish terms means that it flakes easily with a fork when tested, and is neither too wet nor too dry.

◆ The fishy smell on your hands can be removed by rubbing them with some lemon juice when you are finished handling the raw fish.

The Best Gefilte Fish Ever   *Yields 3 medium loaves (or 30 balls)*

Variation:
A generous amount
of paprika, and/or
3–4 whole cloves of
garlic can be added
to the broth when
cooking.

*Tip:
For a broth that
gels, add in 2–3 fish
bones or fish heads
to the pot when
cooking up the fish.
Leave them in when
you place in refrig-
erator, and as it gets
cold, it will gel.

Serving Suggestion:
Cut off the top of a
1/2 liter 1 liter sized
plastic bottle. Place
enough fish batter
inside to fill almost
to the top. Then
push a peeled car-
rot into its center.
Freeze overnight
upright like this.
When ready to
cook, pop out fish
"log" and place into
boiling water. Cook
as directed. When
you slice it there
will be a decorative
carrot in the center
of each piece.

2 1/4 lbs./1 kilo ground fish,
   i.e. carp or cassif (silver carp),
   or a half-half mix; or a mix of
   whitefish and pike
5 whole eggs
2–3 medium carrots, peeled
2 medium onions, peeled
1/2 cup sugar
3 tsp. salt
1 tsp. pepper

Broth ingredients for
   cooking the fish:
1/2 T. salt
3/4 cup sugar
1 onion, peeled and halved
1 carrot, peeled
water
2–3 fish bones or fish heads,
   optional*

Grind carrots and onions in food processor together with 2 of the
eggs. Blend until smooth. Put remaining ingredients into a large
mixer bowl and add the blended vegetable mixture to it. Beat
together for 15 minutes on medium speed until well mixed and a
thick consistency. Cover and place in refrigerator for at least an
hour, or overnight if necessary, before shaping. Can be shaped into
balls and cooked up right away, or frozen into logs for later use.

To Freeze:

Logs: In a medium sized freezer bag, scoop in about 2 cups of fish
batter. Hold bag by top and bang lightly on counter top to even out
the mixture in the bottom of the bag. Roll in bag to form "log"
shape and then place widthwise in a 9x13 inch baking pan, wrap-
ping the empty part of bag under the log. Continue with the
remainder of the batter, forming about 3–4 logs. Place pan in
freezer. When solid, remove from pan and leave in freezer until
ready for use. Boil while log is still frozen.
Balls: Shape the batter into balls with wet hands and drop onto a
cookie sheet lined with baking paper. Allow to freeze overnight
uncovered. When solid, place frozen raw balls into freezer bags.
Boil while balls are still frozen.

(continued on next page)

The Best Gefilte Fish Ever (continued)

To Cook:

Fill a large cooking pot halfway with water. The pot should have room for the fish to expand. Add the ingredients for the broth. When broth is boiling rapidly, add the fish. Cover pot halfway, and turn down flame to simmer for about 1 1/2 hours. If you are using frozen fish logs, follow the same directions for broth and after the water boils, take the log out of the plastic bag while still frozen and place in water. After cooking, place the fish in a large plastic container together with some broth and the vegetables. To keep the fish balls from getting squashed while storing, lay them out in a single layer.

Suggestion:
Make your own "heimishe chrein" on Pesach! Recipe on page 38.

Sweet 'n Sour Fish *Serves 6*

2 1/4 lbs./1 kilo of 2 inch fish steaks of any kind, i.e., salmon, flounder, or Nile perch
1/2 cup water
1/2 cup sugar
1/4 cup (wine) vinegar
1 T. salt
1 T. pickling spices
2 medium onions, sliced

Clean and scale fish pieces and place in a large flat container. Mix the water, sugar, vinegar, salt and pickling spices in a bowl. Pour over fish pieces and let marinate in the fridge overnight. The next day, place the sliced onions on bottom of pot; add the fish with marinade and cook together for 20 minutes on low flame. Let cool and refrigerate. Serve cold.

Carp Just Like Bubby's

Serves 10

10 pieces of carp, cleaned
4 large carrots, peeled and cut
    into chunks
2 large onions, halved
3 garlic cloves. whole

3/4 cup sugar
1 T. salt
3/4 tsp. pepper
2 tsp. paprika
water

Tip:
Clean carp pieces very well by removing the scales from the outside of skin and any guts that may be clinging to the inside of the cavity. Remember to follow directions for checking for bugs in your community when cleaning carp.

Fill the largest pot you have a little more than halfway with water. Start boiling, while adding the onions, carrots, garlic cloves, sugar, and spices. Add in the fish pieces. When broth is boiling, reduce heat to simmer, and cover. Cook like this for 45 minutes to an hour. Transfer fish, broth and vegetables to a container. Cover and refrigerate overnight.

Easy Fancy Yom Tov Stuffed Carp

Serves 4–10

4–10 carp steaks, cleaned

Broth from recipe above

This recipe has a very special Yom Tov look to it and is sure to make you feel like a real balabusta!

Tip:
When ordering the carp pieces, make sure to request steaks that have holes in the middle large enough to be stuffed.

Prepare the "Best Gefilte Fish Ever" recipe from preceding pages and chill batter as directed for several hours or overnight. When batter is chilled, prepare carp. Clean off the steaks and lay on paper towels to dry. Prepare broth for carp fish pieces as stated in above recipe. When broth is already boiling, take each piece of carp and carefully stuff a large handful of the gefilte fish batter into the hole in middle of steak as well as you can. Place into boiling broth immediately after stuffing each piece. Let it cook this way until done, about 1 1/2 hours. Remove fish plus broth and vegetables to a container. Cover and refrigerate overnight.

Note: This recipe can be prepared in advance on the same day you make your gefilte fish, to be frozen and cooked another day. Stuff the carp steaks as listed in directions, then lay them out in a single layer on a cookie sheet lined with baking paper. Freeze open overnight, then place in a heavy duty freezer bag until needed. To boil, prepare broth as usual, then add in fish pieces straight from freezer.

Tender Fish Steaks

Serves 3–4

Suggestion:
For an even tastier dish, mix the lemon juice, olive oil, and spices in a flat container. Rub the marinade well onto both sides of the fish steaks and let marinate for an hour in refrigerator before baking uncovered at 350°F/180°C for 20 minutes.

3–4 salmon or halibut steaks, 1 inch thick, cleaned and scaled
1 small onion, sliced
1 garlic clove, diced
1 stalk celery, diced, optional
2 T. lemon juice

3–4 sprigs each fresh dill and parsley
1/2 tsp. each paprika, onion powder, and garlic powder
1/4 cup water
2 T. olive oil

Heat olive oil in a pan. Add sliced vegetables and saute for about 5 minutes. Add water and cover pan securely with lid. Rub the fish steaks with the lemon juice. Sprinkle spices all over both sides of fish. Place the fish on top of the vegetables in pan and place the sprigs of parsley and dill on the fish. Cover and cook for 15 minutes, taking care that it should not burn. Turn off flame, leave covered, and let it steam in pan another 10 minutes. Serve immediately.

Fish With Vegetables

Serves 4–6

4–6 fish fillets (any non-oily fish such as sole, flounder, salmon, or Nile perch)
1 cup baby carrots or thin carrot slices
1 large red tomato, chopped
1 medium green pepper, diced

1 small onion, diced
1/4 cup freshly squeezed lemon juice
1 T. fresh basil or 1/2 tsp. dried
1 T. fresh parsley or 1/2 tsp. dried
2 T. white wine

Place fillets in shallow baking dish, lined with baking paper. Dice up the vegetables, combine with the other ingredients, and spoon over the fillets. Cover the baking dish and bake at 400°F/200°C for 10–15 minutes until done.

Stovetop Directions:

Follow same directions as baking, placing everything in a large and deep frying pan that has a well fitting cover. Cook on low flame until done, about 15–20 minutes. Serve hot, covering the fish with vegetables and pan juices on the plate.

Non-Gebrochs "Breaded" Fish   *Serves 4–6*

2 1/4 lbs./1 kilo any white fish, filleted
    or sliced into 2 inch thick pieces,
    i.e., Nile perch, sole, flounder,
    baccala (whiting)
1 onion
2 garlic cloves

3 eggs or 5 egg whites
1/2 cup potato starch
1/2 tsp. each onion powder, garlic
    powder, paprika
1/4 tsp. pepper
olive oil

Tip:
The fish may stick
somewhat to the
pan so make sure
you keep it greased,
and that you
remove it gently
with a spatula when
taking it out.

Wash off fish and pat dry slightly before "breading". Mix potato starch in a bowl together with a bit of water until it forms a thin paste, then add the eggs and mix again. Puree the onions and garlic in food processor until almost liquid and add to potato starch mixture. Add spices to taste. Mix all together to form a thick, but not solid, paste. Heat up olive oil in large frying pan. Coat each piece of fish with the mixture, and fry immediately or else mixture will separate. Fry on medium flame for 15 minutes per side, or until nicely browned. Can be served hot or cold.

Mayonnaise Fish   *Serves 4*

6 2 inch thick white fish fillets such as
    flounder, sole, or Nile perch
3 T. onion powder, or 1 large onion,
    pureed

1 cup mayonnaise
garlic powder
paprika

Remove any scales or skin from fish fillets, wash off, and lay flat in a baking pan or dish. Mix together rest of ingredients, except paprika, in a bowl until smooth. Spread the mixture all over the fish. Sprinkle generously with paprika. Bake uncovered in oven at 400°F/200°C until done, about 10–15 minutes. Serve while still hot.

FISH

Note:
See photograph on
page 27

Serving Suggestion:
Place on serving
platter whole, on a
bed of fresh lettuce
with other vegeta-
bles around it.

Roasted Garlic Fish   *Serves 4*

*1 whole fish such as buri, St. Peter's,
    or sea bass, cleaned, split open and
    insides removed*
9 garlic cloves, peeled

juice of 1 lemon
1/3 cup olive oil
*1 small bunch each fresh parsley
    and dill*

Preheat oven to broil on 400°F/200°C. Line a 9x13 inch pan with
baking paper. Pat fish dry with paper towels and lay in the pan.
Smear the fish inside and out generously with olive oil. Stuff the
insides with the fresh parsley and dill. Slice the garlic cloves and
place into the cavity of the fish as well. Drizzle lemon juice over
fish, inside and out. Bake uncovered for about 20 minutes. If not
serving immediately, remove from oven and cover with foil. Let sit
on counter until serving.

Tuna Salad   *Serves 4*

2 cans (6 oz. each can) tuna, drained
2 small scallions, diced
1 stalk celery, diced
2 T. walnuts, chopped, optional
2 hard boiled egg whites, diced
1 tomato, diced

1 cucumber, diced
2 pickles, diced
2 T. mayonnaise
1/2 tsp. garlic powder, optional
1/2 tsp. lemon juice

Place all ingredients in a large bowl and mix well together. For a
creamier consistency, blend the tuna, eggs, spices, lemon juice and
mayonnaise in food processor until smooth. Then add in the diced
ingredients. Serve immediately or refrigerate several hours.

Fish Roll-Ups

Serves 6

6–10 sole or flounder fillets
3–4 medium potatoes
1 large onion
1 tsp. salt

1/2 tsp. pepper
1 (15 oz.) can tomato sauce or
    5 fresh tomatoes, pureed
olive oil

Preheat oven to 350°F/180°C. Peel potatoes, cut into chunks and boil until soft. Saute onion in olive oil. Mash potatoes and combine with sauteed onion. Season with salt and pepper. On a separate

dish, lay fillets flat and spoon potatoes on one end of the fillet. Roll up fillet lengthwise and place seam side down in a baking pan lined with parchment paper. Top with tomato sauce and bake covered for 35–40 minutes.

Stovetop Directions:
Follow same directions, and place fillets in large frying pan with lid. Top with sauce and simmer on low flame until done, about 25–30 minutes, taking care it does not burn. Serve hot.

Oriental Tuna

Serves 2

1 can (6 oz.) tuna, drained
1 green pepper, cut into thin strips
1 small onion, thinly sliced
2 tsp. oil
2/3 cup canned pineapple chunks,
    drained

1/3 cup pineapple juice
1 tsp. potato starch
1 T. water
1 T. (wine) vinegar
  pinch pepper
1 T. sugar

Saute green pepper and onion in oil until soft. In a small bowl, mix potato starch with water until a paste is formed. Then add in pineapple juice and stir so no lumps will form. Add this to sauteed vegetables. Cook together, stirring gently, until thick. Add remaining ingredients and cook for 5 more minutes. May be served alone or over mashed potatoes.

FISH

Mock Salmon Spread

Serves 6

Suggestion:
Serve as a scoop on top of lettuce, with cucumber and carrot rounds for garnish.

2.5 lb./1 kilo Nile perch, flounder, sole or baccala (whiting), cleaned
3/4 cup mayonnaise
3/4 cup tomato sauce, or 5 fresh tomatoes, pureed
1 tsp. salt

1/2 tsp. pepper
1 T. sugar
2 T. (wine) vinegar
1 T. lemon juice
1 small onion, diced

Place fish in large pot with water to cover and boil for 25 minutes until cooked. Remove any bones from fish and place in food processor together with all other ingredients except the onion. Puree until smooth. Remove and place in a plastic container. Mix in the diced onion. Refrigerate overnight before serving.

Heimishe Chrein

Yields 2–2 1/2 cups

Note:
Keep in mind that the horseradish root tends to lose some of its sharpness once it sits after being grated, so you could wait until the next day to adjust the taste.

3 T. freshly grated horseradish root
4 medium sized beets
1 tsp. salt

4 T. sugar
2 T. (wine) vinegar
2–3 T. beet water

Peel and wash off beets very well. Cut into large chunks and place in pot. Cover with water and boil until soft, about 1 hour. Drain the beets, reserving 2–3 T. beet water. Puree the beets and mix together with horseradish root. Add the remaining ingredients and let it sit covered in refrigerator for 2–3 hours. Adjust to taste. For a sweet taste, add more sugar; for a mild taste, add more beets; for a strong taste, add more horseradish root. Add them each a little at a time as it can become overpowering very quickly. Refrigerate before serving.

NOTES TO REMEMBER

Meat & Poultry

Tangy Meat Roast, page 44

Apricot Meat Roast

Serves 8

4–6 lbs./2–3 kilo end of steak roast,
   or any meat roast
2 onions, diced
6 garlic cloves, diced
2/3 cup apricot preserves

1 cup semi-dry red wine
1 cup water
1/2 tsp. pepper
2 bay leaves, optional
1 tsp. parsley

Prepare this recipe the day before you plan on serving it. Trim excess fat off roast. Combine remaining ingredients in a bowl and mix well. Place meat in roasting pan; pour mixture on top. Cover well and bake for 3 hours at 350°F/180°C, basting occasionally. Refrigerate overnight. Remove roast from pan, reserving the juices, and slice. Then return meat to pan and cover with juices. Cover and bake again before serving for another 1–2 hours.

Stovetop Directions:
Follow directions for preparing as above and cook on low heat for 3 hours. Refrigerate. After slicing, return to pot with original juices and cook for at least another hour, until tender.

Meat Roast in Wine

Serves 6–8

4–5 lbs./2–3 kilo any meat roast
2 large onions, sliced
3–5 garlic cloves, diced
2 cups dry or semi-dry white wine

pepper, paprika, onion powder, and
garlic powder to taste
1 cup water

Line bottom of a pot with half of the onion and the garlic cloves. Rub the roast well with one more piece of garlic all over, then season with spices liberally on all sides. Place roast in pan on top of onions. Pour water and wine over roast. Sprinkle more paprika on top of roast, and add rest of onions. Cover pot and cook on a low flame for 3 hours. Remove from heat and refrigerate overnight. Remove roast from pan, reserving the juices, and slice. Return meat to pan, cover with juices, and cook for another 1–2 hours.

Hint:
The larger a roast is the juicier it will be.

Tip:
Roasts tend to slice much easier when cold.

Variation:
Sliced dried, fresh, or canned apricots can be added before reheating the second time.

Note:
See photograph on page 41

Tangy Veal or Meat Roast

Serves 8–10

4–5 lbs./2–3 kilo roast,
*   washed and dried*
1 cup semi-dry white wine
1/4 cup olive oil
1/4 cup (wine) vinegar
6 garlic cloves, peeled
2 T. parsley flakes
1/2 tsp. oregano

Next Day Marinade:
1/2 cup olive oil
1/2 cup (wine) vinegar
1 T. parsley flakes
1/2 tsp. oregano
1 cup tomato sauce, optional
6–8 garlic cloves, pressed
3 stalks celery, diced
3 carrots, sliced into rounds
2 large onions, sliced

In a bowl, squeeze the garlic cloves with a garlic press. Add olive oil, vinegar, and spices to bowl, mixing well. Place meat into large glass or plastic container and pour this garlic mixture over it. Marinate for 6 hours or overnight, basting periodically. Then place meat in a pot that fits its size as closely as possible. Add the wine to the meat and simmer for 3 hours. Refrigerate overnight.

The next day, remove the meat from pot and discard the juices. Slice and lay flat into a 9x13 inch (or a bit larger) baking pan. Mix up ingredients for next day marinade and pour over meat slices. Cut up vegetables and arrange over the meat slices. Cover well with foil and bake in oven at 350°F/180°C for another 2 hours, basting once an hour or so to prevent from drying out.

Pepper Short Ribs

Serves 6

4–5 lbs./2–3 kilo short ribs, or flanken
6 green peppers, sliced
1 large onion, diced small
3 T. sugar

1 T. potato starch
1 cup dry or semi-dry white wine
olive oil
water

Saute the green peppers with a bit of olive oil in a covered pot until soft. Remove from pot and refrigerate. Then wash the short ribs well and slice into large chunks. In a pot, brown meat on both sides. Reduce heat to low and add diced onion. Add 3 T. water and wine to ribs in pot. Cover and simmer for 8–9 hours, checking and basting occasionally. After cooking, remove ribs from pot, reserving juices. In a small bowl, mix together 1 T. water, sugar, and potato starch until smooth. Combine with reserved juices and heat, stirring until thick. Add the green peppers from the refrigerator to the liquid and then return the meat to pot. Simmer for another 1/2 hour or so. If the sauce gets too thick you may add a bit more water or wine to it.

Tip:
Do not cut meat pieces too small as they shrink in cooking, and will also dry out much more.

Suggestion:
The sauce is delicious served over potato or chicken blintzes as well.
Recipe for blintze and filling can be found on pages 65–66.

Meat Roast Tasty Style

Serves 6–8

5–8 lbs./2–4 kilo brisket
1–2 scallions
2 medium onions
4 garlic cloves

1 small green pepper
paprika
pepper
2 cups semi-dry white wine

Puree scallions, 1 onion, 3 garlic cloves, and green pepper in food processor. Set aside. Slice remaining onion in half rings, and dice last clove of garlic. Layer in bottom of pot. Sprinkle paprika and a small amount of pepper all over meat and place in pan on top of onions. Pour pureed vegetables all over meat roast. Add wine, cover, and cook on low flame for 4 hours. Refrigerate overnight. Remove meat from pot, leaving all that remained on top of it as is, and slice. Place back into pot and simmer for 2 hours before serving.

Cholent

Serves 6–8

3–4 lbs./ 1.5–2 kilo meat, chicken
    pieces, and/or turkey necks
3 cholent bones
2 large onions
4 garlic cloves

1–2 large potatoes, grated
4–6 potatoes, chopped
1 T. paprika
1/2 tsp. pepper
water

Cut up onions and garlic and saute in bottom of pot. Add in all the meat pieces, brown for a few minutes, and cover with water. Sprinkle in paprika and pepper. Take the grated potatoes and add into the water. Then add the chopped potatoes on top of mixture, sprinkling more paprika on top. Let cook for at least 3 hours before putting on blech.

Turkey and Wine Roast

Serves 6

5 lbs./2.5 kilo white turkey breast
    (some butchers call it a
    "butterfly")
2 large onions, sliced
3–4 garlic cloves, diced

1 small can mushrooms, optional
1/2 tsp. pepper
2 tsp. paprika
2 cups dry or semi-dry white wine

Wash off the roast. Choose a pot that fits the size of the roast and that has a top that seals well. Place half of the onions and garlic on bottom of pot, along with the mushrooms. Place roast bottom side up on vegetables, and pour in wine. Sprinkle roast on all sides with spices. Add remaining vegetables on top of roast and cover tightly. Bring to a boil, then simmer on stovetop for 2 hours. Refrigerate overnight. The next day remove from pot, slice, and return to pot with all the juices. Simmer for another half hour or until heated. Serve hot alone or with mashed potatoes.

Chicken Cacciatore

Serves 6

1 1/2 chickens, skinned and cut up
1 large onion, sliced thin
2–3 garlic cloves, diced
1 tsp. oregano
1 tsp. basil
1/2 tsp. pepper
2 bay leaves

1–2 T. dried parsley flakes
1 cup tomato sauce or
   5–7 fresh tomatoes, pureed
1 cup dry or semi-dry white wine
1 cup water
4 potatoes, peeled
2 T. oil

Brown chicken in oil in a deep frying pan with lid, together with the onions and garlic. Add spices and continue to cook for a few minutes. Mix together the tomato sauce, wine and water and then add to pot. Cover and simmer for 45 minutes. Cut potatoes into small chunks and add to pan. Continue cooking until soft, about another 30 minutes.

Chicken in Wine

Serves 4

1 chicken, skinned and cut up
1 onion, diced
3 garlic cloves, diced
2–3 large carrots, peeled and diced
1 1/2 T. potato starch
1 tsp. marjoram

1/2 tsp. thyme
1/4 tsp. pepper
2 T. dried parsley flakes
1 bay leaf
1 cup dry or semi-dry white wine
2 T. oil

Place diced vegetables in a deep frying pan with lid and saute for 5 minutes. Push vegetables to the sides and brown the chicken. Mix together the potato starch and spices and then sprinkle over the chicken. Simmer covered for 15 minutes or so until the mixture is absorbed into chicken. Pour wine over all and let simmer on stove-top about another hour, until tender.

Chicken Paprikash I

Serves 4

1 large chicken, skinned and cut up
1 green pepper, diced
1–2 large onions, diced
1/2 tsp. pepper
1 tsp. paprika
1–2 T. parsley flakes

1/4 tsp. salt
1 cup tomato sauce
   or 5–7 fresh tomatoes, pureed
1 1/4 cups water
2 T. oil

Place vegetables in bottom of pan with oil and saute for 5 minutes. Push aside vegetables and brown chicken on both sides. Sprinkle the spices over the chicken then cover and simmer chicken about 1/2 hour. Add tomato sauce and water. Continue to simmer another hour. May be served with boiled potatoes.

Chicken Paprikash II

Serves 6

1 1/2 chickens, skinned and cut up
3 large onions, diced
4–5 garlic cloves, diced
1/2–1 cup potato starch, as needed
1 T. paprika
1 tsp. onion powder

1 tsp. garlic powder
1/2 tsp. pepper
1/8 tsp. salt
2 T. olive oil
1–2 cups water or semi-dry white wine
additional paprika

Saute onions and garlic in bottom of large pan in olive oil. Place potato starch and all spices except salt in a plastic bag. Add chicken parts to bag and shake well to coat evenly. Push aside onions and brown the chicken on both sides. May need to keep adding olive oil to pan as potato starch tends to get very sticky. Remove browned chicken pieces and add liquid to the leftover mixture in pan. Stir until it becomes a sauce. Add more paprika and salt to this sauce. Return chicken to pan and simmer until fork tender, about one hour.

Chicken Paprikash II

Chicken Fricassee

Serves 4

1 large chicken, skinned and cut up
1 1/2 cups dry or semi-dry white wine
1 large onion, diced
2 garlic cloves, diced
2–3 stalks celery, diced
2 T. dried parsley flakes

1 T. paprika
1/2 tsp. pepper
1/4 cup potato starch
2 T. oil

Put potato starch in plastic bag with pepper. Place chicken pieces in bag and shake well to coat lightly. Brown chicken in oil in a large pan. Remove chicken from oil and then saute vegetables until soft. Sprinkle parsley flakes and paprika over all and mix. Pour in wine and return chicken to pan. Cover and simmer on stovetop until fork tender, about 1 1/4 hours.

Suggestion:
This recipe can be used to make "breaded" chicken. Follow the same directions, then bake covered until chicken is fork tender, about 1 1/4 hours.

Tip:
For a reduced fat recipe, you may fry each piece just for a few minutes on each side. Then transfer to a pan lined with baking paper, cover it well, and bake at 350°F/ 180°C for 35–40 minutes until done.

"Breaded" Cutlets

Serves 4

2 1/4 lbs./1 kilo chicken or turkey cutlets
5 eggs or 5 egg whites
2 large onions
3 garlic cloves
1/4 cup water

4 T. potato starch
1/2 tsp. salt
large dash paprika
1/4–1/2 tsp. pepper
oil for frying

Pound cutlets out to preferred thinness on a board. Lightly beat eggs in a large bowl. Puree onions and garlic in the food processor; set aside. In a separate bowl stir water and potato starch until almost smooth. Add starch mixture to the eggs in bowl and mix together. Add in spices and the pureed vegetables, mixing well again. If the mixture is too thin, add a bit more potato starch to it until it resembles a loose paste. In a large frying pan, heat enough oil to coat the pan plus a bit extra. Coat each piece of cutlet with the mixture, and fry immediately or else mixture will separate. Fry on both sides until golden brown, about 15 minutes per side.

Chicken Fricassee

Moussaka I

Serves 6

2 large eggplant, washed well or
  peeled
salt for sprinkling
5 garlic cloves, diced
1 large onion, diced
olive oil
1 lb./1/2 kilo ground turkey
1/2 tsp. pepper
1/2 tsp. salt
2 potatoes, cooked and mashed

Sauce:
1 cup tomato paste or 5–7 fresh
  tomatoes, peeled and pureed
1 cup hot water
1/2 cup white or brown sugar
1 1/2 tsp. salt
1/2 tsp. pepper

Cut off stems and slice eggplant the long way. Sprinkle salt on the slices and let sit for 10 minutes. Rinse well and pat dry. Fry eggplant slices in olive oil or layer in a roasting pan with oil on both sides and bake at 350°F/180°C until light brown. Remove from pan and set aside.

Saute diced onion and garlic in olive oil for about 10 minutes. Then add in meat and brown it, mixing well every few minutes. Let meat simmer for a total of 30 minutes. Then add in the mashed potatoes and sprinkle salt and pepper over all.

Line a 9x13 inch pan with baking paper. Arrange one layer of eggplant on the bottom, spread the meat mixture evenly over all, then layer rest of eggplant. Mix together ingredients for sauce and pour evenly over top. Cover with foil and bake at 350°F/180°C for 45 minutes. Uncover and bake for another 15 minutes. Cuts nicely after being refrigerated overnight first.

Suggestion:
For a quick side dish, layer any yellow vegetables, i.e., sweet potatoes, acorn squash, or butternut squash under the chicken, and the juices from the chicken will enhance the taste of the vegetables.

Quick 'n Easy Glazed Chicken

Serves 4–8

1–2 chickens, skinned and cut up
1 cup apricot jam
3/4 cup mayonnaise

1 cup Pesachdik ketchup
3 T. Pesachdik onion soup mix

Mix all ingredients together well and spread over chicken. Bake covered for 1 1/2 hours, until fork tender.

Moussaka II

Serves 6

2 large eggplant, washed well or
  peeled
salt for sprinkling
1 onion, chopped
2 T. olive oil
1 lb./1/2 kilo ground meat or turkey
2 garlic cloves
1/2 cup water
1/2 tsp. oregano
1/2 tsp. thyme
1/4 tsp. cinnamon
1/4 tsp. pepper
1 cup tomato paste or 5–7 fresh
tomatoes, peeled and pureed

White Sauce:
2 T. oil
2 T. potato starch
1 1/4 cups water
2 eggs
1/2 tsp. salt
1/2 tsp. nutmeg, optional

Cut off stems and slice eggplant the long way. Sprinkle salt on the slices and let sit for 10 minutes. Rinse well and pat dry. Place slices on a baking sheet and drizzle with oil and bake at 350°F/180°C until light brown. Remove from oven.

Saute onions and garlic for 10 minutes. Add in meat or turkey and brown, mixing well. Lower the flame and simmer for 30 minutes. Add spices and tomato paste. Add water, mix well and continue simmering another 5–10 minutes.

To prepare sauce, dissolve starch in oil, mixing well, and add water. Lightly beat eggs. Then add 2 T. of the starch mixture to the beaten eggs, mix, and then combine this mixture with original mixture. Add everything else and set aside.

Line a 9x13 inch pan with baking paper. Put one layer of eggplant down, spread meat mixture evenly over all, then top with rest of eggplant. Cover with the white sauce and bake uncovered at 325°F/170°C for 45 minutes–1 hour. If you make it a day ahead, you can slice it more easily after it's been refrigerated overnight, and then reheat covered.

Mrs. Buxbaum's Falshe Fish

Yields 40–50 balls

This traditional recipe of "imitation" fish began many generations ago. Although today there are many types of fish available for Pesach, Falshe Fish remains a favorite in many households.

Tip:
The chicken bones in the broth will give an excellent taste and cause it to become jelled when cooled.

Tip:
Straining the broth through a cheese-cloth after cooking makes it look nice and clear.

3 lbs./1.5 kilo ground chicken breast
4 eggs
1 large onion, grated
1 carrot, grated
1/2 cup seltzer or water
1 cup sugar
1 T. salt
4 large potatoes, cooked and mashed
*   very finely (with a potato masher)*

Broth:
4 quarts water
2.5 lb./1 kilo chicken bones
3 large onions sliced
3 carrots sliced
2 cups sugar
2 T salt
1 tsp. pepper
1–2 pieces dried gingeroot, optional

Combine all ingredients for the falshe fish. Refrigerate for 1 hour or more. In a 12–14 quart pot, bring all ingredients for broth to a boil. With wet hands shape the falshe fish mixture into balls and drop in boiling broth. Cook for 1 1/2 hours over low to medium heat.

Chopped Liver

Serves 6

1 lb./1/2 kilo kashered chicken livers
5–6 hard boiled eggs
*   (depending on taste)*
2 large onions

1–2 tsp. salt
1/2 tsp. pepper
3 T. mayonnaise, optional

Slice onions in half rings and saute in a bit of oil until brown. Place liver in food processor. Add the onions, eggs, and spices. Puree together until very smooth. Add mayonnaise for a smoother consistency. Can be frozen in portions or used right away. Stays for about 3 days in fridge.

Stuffed Cabbage, Regular Style

Serves 10–15

This recipe is only for those people who use canned goods on Pesach. If you do not, refer instead to the next Stuffed Cabbage recipe. See also step by step instructions for filling and rolling cabbage in the next cabbage recipe.

1 lb./1/2 kilo ground chicken
1 lb./1/2 kilo ground red meat
2 eggs or 3 egg whites
1 large onion
1 grated potato
1 1/2 T. salt

2 T. sugar
1 1/2 tsp. pepper, divided
2 T. lemon juice
2 cups tomato paste and 4 cups water
large head of green cabbage

A day or two before starting, place cabbage head in freezer. The night before you want to make this, remove it and let it defrost on the countertop in a bowl. It will emit a lot of water while defrosting and may also smell funny; this is normal. This action will replace the process of cooking the cabbage to soften the leaves for easy separation. Dice onions and place in a bowl. Add in both meats, the grated potato, eggs, and 3/4 tsp. pepper. Mix together very well. Peel off cabbage leaves one at a time and place a tablespoon or so of the meat mixture in its center. Roll up tightly. Place in layers in the bottom of your empty pot until all the cabbage is used up. In a bowl, mix the tomato paste and water, together with the lemon juice, sugar, and salt and another 3/4 tsp. pepper. Pour over cabbage rolls. Bring to a boil, then turn down flame and allow to simmer for at least 5 hours. Freezes well.

Variation:
For both stuffed cabbage recipes, if you have neither the time nor the patience to "stuff" the cabbage, try this method instead. Using a sharp knife, slice the cabbage head thinly and place on the bottom of large pot. Prepare the sauce and set it to cook. Make the meat mixture and roll into balls. Add to the sauce. Follow the same cooking time for your very own "Cabbage Meatballs" instead!

*Note:
Prepare cabbage head in advance as directed in recipe for "Regular Style" on previous page.

Stuffed Cabbage, Homemade Style

Serves 10–15

1 lb./1/2 kilo ground chicken
1 lb./1/2 kilo ground red meat
1 potato, grated
2 eggs or 3 egg whites
3 large onions
3/4 cup sugar
1 1/2 cups water
1 T. vinegar

Step-by-Step

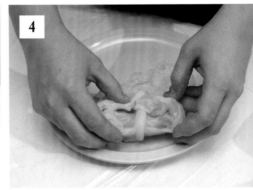

8 large tomatoes, peeled
2 T. lemon juice
1 green pepper
5–7 garlic cloves, optional
1 1/2 T. salt
3/4 tsp. pepper
large head of green cabbage *

Puree 2 large onions, tomatoes, green pepper, and garlic in your food processor. Set aside. In a very large pot, pour in the sugar and brown it over a small flame until it is liquidy. Then add water to it and mix well, keeping it liquidy. Add in the vinegar and lemon juice. Add the vegetable mixture to the pot. Cook together for about 30 minutes until it turns saucy. In a large bowl, mix together the meats, spices, grated potato, eggs, and the last onion, diced small. Peel off cabbage leaves one at a time and fill them with a tablespoon or so of the meat mixture (**see 1,2**). Roll once turn towards you. Fold in the right side, then the left side; then continue rolling until it is completely rolled (**see 3,4,5**). As you finish each roll, add it to the sauce in the pot (**see 6**). Simmer at least 6–7 hours. The longer you cook it the more flavor it will have. Freezes well.

Tip:
You can add any leftover meat as meatballs to the pot, but only after the sauce has started boiling. If you have leftover cabbage pieces, add them as well.

MEAT & POULTRY

Lemon and Garlic Chicken   *Serves 6*

1 1/2 chickens, skinned and cut up
6 garlic cloves, peeled
3 T. lemon juice
1/3 cup chicken soup

1 T. grated lemon peel,
*   or another 1 T. lemon juice*
2 tsp. oregano
1 tsp. thyme

Cut one garlic clove in half and rub chicken pieces on both sides. Place chicken in roasting pan upside down. Dice or squeeze in garlic press 3 garlic cloves and sprinkle over chicken. Slice the remaining 2 cloves in halves or quarters and stuff into whatever crevices in the chicken you find. Mix the 3 T. lemon juice and chicken soup together and pour over all. Add seasonings. Cover and bake at 350°F/180°C for 1/2 hour. Turn over chicken pieces, baste, and continue to bake for another 45 minutes until done. May be served with chunky boiled potatoes.

Olive 'n Spice Chicken   *Serves 4*

1 chicken, skinned and cut up
1 tsp. garlic powder
1 tsp. onion powder
1/8 tsp. pepper
1/2 tsp. cumin
1/2 tsp. thyme
1 T. Italian spices or oregano

1 T. parsley flakes
4 T. lemon juice
a handful of sliced olives
1 medium onion, finely chopped
2 stalks celery, finely chopped
1 cup semi-dry white wine
1 cup chicken soup

Lay chicken pieces upside down on bottom of 9x13 inch pan. Sprinkle with garlic powder, onion powder, pepper and thyme. Pour lemon juice over all. Turn pieces over and add the chicken soup and wine. Sprinkle with the cumin, Italian spices, and parsley flakes. Add onion, celery, and olives over the top of chicken pieces. Bake at 375°F/190°C for one hour.

Chicken Italiano

Serves 6

1 1/2 chickens, skinned and cut up	*1 T. parsley flakes*
1/4 cup potato starch	*1 T. Italian spice, optional*
1/2 cup sliced olive rings	*1/2 tsp. marjoram*
1 medium onion, red or white, diced	*1/2 tsp. thyme*
2 garlic cloves, minced	*1/4 tsp. pepper*
1 small red pepper, sliced	*1 tsp. sugar*
1 small green pepper, sliced	*1 T. (wine) vinegar*
1 medium tomato, cubed	*olive oil*
1 1/2 cups semi-dry white wine	

Cover bottom of large skillet with olive oil, and shake chicken pieces in bag with potato starch to coat evenly. Brown chicken parts in the oil on both sides. Remove from pan. Add onion, garlic, peppers, and tomato to the remains in pot. Add wine and vinegar, and stir for a minute. Add olive rings and then place chicken on top of all. Combine all spices together in a bowl and then sprinkle over chicken. Simmer on stovetop covered for one hour, until fork tender.

Orange Chicken

Serves 4–6

1–1 1/2 chickens, skinned and cut up
2 T. olive oil
2 large onions, sliced
3 garlic cloves, diced
1 T. paprika
1/2 tsp. pepper

4 stalks celery, diced
3 large carrots, cut into rounds
1 green pepper, diced
1 cup orange juice
1 cup dry or semi-dry white wine

Saute onions and garlic in olive oil until clear. Place half of them on bottom of a pot. Place chicken on top, upside down, and sprinkle liberally with half of the paprika and pepper. Add other half of onions and garlic on top of chicken, together with remaining vegetables. Pour orange juice and wine over all. Let marinate in refrigerator for several hours or overnight before cooking. Cover and bake at 375°F/190°C until fork tender, about 1 hour.

Scallion 'n Mushroom Chicken

Serves 6

1 1/2 chickens, skinned and cut up
1/4 cup potato starch
1/2 tsp. seasoned salt
1/4 tsp. pepper
1 tsp. paprika
1 tsp. each garlic and onion powder
2 T. oil
3 large scallions
1 large onion

1 cup fresh or canned mushrooms, sliced
2 garlic cloves, optional
1 green pepper
2 T. potato starch
1 large glass dry white wine
3/4 cup tomato sauce or 4–5 fresh
tomatoes, pureed
2 T. parsley flakes
large dash paprika

Place 1/4 cup potato starch and first 4 spices in a plastic bag. Shake chicken in bag to coat evenly and brown in the oil on both sides. Remove from pan, reserving the juices. Add a bit more oil and saute the scallions, onion, garlic, mushrooms and green pepper for 5–10 minutes until just getting soft. Add 2 T. potato starch and mix well. Pour in the wine and tomato sauce and sprinkle in last 2 ingredients. Mix well and add chicken pieces. Simmer until fork tender, about 1 1/4 hours.

Notes to Remember

Side Dishes
& Cooked Salads

Stuffed Squash, page 76

Blintzes

Yields 12–14

4 whole eggs
1/4 cup potato starch
1/3 cup water

Beat all of the ingredients together until smooth. Place in refrigerator for a few hours. Remove bubbles from the top of the mixture before frying. Stir mixture by hand if it has settled. Heat some oil in a frying pan, or use a non-stick pan. When oil is hot, pour in some batter, and rotating the pan, spread the batter evenly around the bottom of it. Fry for about a minute. As the blintze begins to curl, remove from pan, and flip onto a plate. Continue with remaining batter. Fill immediately because they turn moldy if left in refrigerator for too long. After filling them, they can be served right away or frozen for later use.* To reheat before serving, you can refry them in a pan on both sides.

*Tip:
Once the blintzes are filled, you may freeze them flat on a cookie sheet until frozen, then place in freezer bags for use at a later time.

Fillings:

✦ **Potato Blintzes:** Peel and boil 8 potatoes until soft, about 40 minutes, and mash, adding small amount of oil, and salt and pepper to taste. Dice and saute one large onion, until soft and brown. Add the sauteed onions to the mashed potatoes and mix all together. Fill blintzes with spoonfuls of mixture and roll up. Freezes well.

✦ **Mushroom Blintzes:** Saute one box of fresh mushrooms and two large onions, cut into half rings, until onions are very soft. Add a dash of salt and pepper to flavor it. For a thicker consistency, mix 1/2 tsp. potato starch and 3 T. water in a bowl, stir until smooth, and add to the sauteing vegetables. Fill blintzes with spoonfuls of mixture and roll up. Freezes well.

Tip:
Follow the step-by-step instructions for "Stuffed Cabbage" on page 56. It works the same way..

(continued on next page)

Blintze Fillings: (continued)

✦ **Chicken/Tuna Blintzes:** Dice and saute a variety of vegetables, such as onions, green pepper, several stalks celery, garlic, and mushrooms in 2 T. oil. When almost done, add salt and pepper to taste, and one or two cans of tuna, or cooked chicken cut into small pieces, whichever you are making. You can thicken the mixture by adding in 1/2 tsp. potato starch mixed with 3 T. water. Stir well. Fill blintzes with spoonfuls of mixture and roll up.

Tip:
This is a great way to use up all that soup chicken left over from your Seder nights.

✦ **Cheese Blintzes:** Mix together ingredients below and fill the blintzes. If you freeze them, refry while still somewhat frozen before serving.

1 cup sour cream or farmer's cheese, or 2 containers 5% Israeli white cheese

1 cup cottage cheese, or another container of same Israeli 5% cheese as above

1/2 cup sugar

1 packet vanilla sugar or 2 tsp. vanilla extract

2 tsp. cinnamon

1/2 cup raisins, optional

Blintze Sauces:

✦ **Vegetable Sauce:** Dice and saute vegetables such as onions, garlic, green pepper, celery, and mushrooms in 2 T. oil. Add 1/2 cup water, 1/4 tsp. salt and a dash of pepper. Put 1 tsp. potato starch in bowl with a bit more water, stir until smooth, and add to cooking mixture on stovetop. Stir and keep stirring until smooth and not too thick. If too thin, add more potato starch; if too thick, add more water. Adding a little at a time is the trick to this sauce. Taste for salt adjustment. Serve hot over blintzes.

✦ **Meat Vegetable Sauce:** Use the leftover sauce from "Pepper Short Ribs" found on page 45. You can add even more vegetables to the sauce when it's cooking. Serve hot over the potato or chicken blintzes.

Mushroom Blintzes with Vegetable Sauce

Eggplant Dip

Serves 6

1 medium-large firm eggplant
3 T. olive oil
4–5 onions, diced
3 garlic cloves, diced
1 box mushrooms, cleaned and sliced

1 green pepper, diced
1 red pepper, diced
1–2 tsp. lemon juice
1 tsp. salt
1/4 tsp. pepper

Wrap the eggplant in foil and bake at 350°F/180°C until soft, about 45 minutes. Meanwhile, heat olive oil in a pan large enough for all vegetables and saute the onions, garlic, mushrooms, and peppers until soft. When eggplant is soft, remove from foil and scoop out all the insides, discarding the peel and as many seeds as possible. Put through food processor together with the sauteed vegetables. Add the lemon juice, salt and pepper. Blend thoroughly. Refrigerate for several hours or overnight.

Carrot Tzimmes

Serves 4–6

1 bag frozen baby carrots
1/4 cup white or light brown sugar
1/2 cup golden raisins
10 prunes, optional

1 cup pineapple pieces, optional
1 tsp. potato starch liquidized
    with 3 T. water

Place carrots in a covered pot and cook on a low flame in a small amount of water until soft, about 2–3 hours. Periodically check that the carrots do not run out of water and burn. Add the sugar and let it simmer for another 10 minutes. Add in the raisins, prunes, and pineapple. Stir in the potato starch mixture. The tzimmes will thicken almost immediately. Turn off flame. Serve warm.

Cold Eggplant Salad

Serves 6–8

1 large onion, diced
2 garlic cloves, diced
1 green pepper, diced
1 firm eggplant, peeled and cubed
4 T. olive oil
1 tsp. salt

1/2 tsp. pepper
1/2 tsp. oregano, optional
1 T. sugar
2 T. (wine) vinegar
3/4 cup tomato sauce or 4–5 fresh
tomatoes, pureed

Heat oil in a 4 qt. saucepan. Layer in order the onion, garlic, pepper and cubed eggplant. Saute for about 10 minutes on a low flame. Add seasonings, sugar and vinegar, then tomato sauce. Mix until all vegetables are evenly coated. Cover pan and simmer for an additional 35 minutes. Chill before serving.

Olive and Mushroom Salad

Serves 4

2 large onions, cut into half rings
3 garlic cloves, minced
1 red pepper, sliced thin
1 green pepper, sliced thin
1 medium tomato, cubed, optional
1/3 cup olives, pitted or in rings

1 small can mushrooms, or one
    box fresh mushrooms,
    cleaned and sliced
1/4 cup olive oil
1/2 cup tomato paste
1 tsp. salt
1/8 tsp. pepper

Place oil in pan, and layer onions, garlic, peppers, olives, tomato, and mushrooms. Cover pan and simmer for 20 minutes until soft. Add tomato paste, salt, and pepper, and continue to simmer for another 20 minutes. Serve warm or cold.

Tomato, Eggplant, and Zucchini Salad

Serves 8

Variations:
1. Chopped leeks can be added to the onions when sauteing for a different taste.
2. Shredded mozzarella cheese can be added between the vegetables and to the top.

2 garlic cloves, minced
1 eggplant, peeled and diced
5 large zucchini, scrubbed and diced
2 large onions, red or white,
    sliced thin in half rounds
1 green pepper, diced
1 red pepper, diced
5 tomatoes, skinned and sliced thin

1/3 cup olive oil
1/2 tsp. salt
1/8 tsp. pepper
1 T. sugar
1 T. fresh basil or 1/2 tsp. dried
1 T. fresh tarragon or 1/2 tsp. dried
1 tsp. oregano
1 T. (wine) vinegar

Oven: Heat olive oil in pan and saute vegetables, excluding the tomatoes, for about 8–10 minutes. Mix together the spices and sugar in a small bowl. Then in bottom of baking dish, layer half the tomatoes,then the sauteed vegetables, and sprinkle with half the seasonings. Then layer the remaining tomato slices and vinegar and sprinkle other half of seasonings over the top. Cover and bake for about 25 minutes at 325°F/170°C, until hot and bubbly. Serve warm.

Stovetop: Heat oil in pan and saute vegetables until tender, leaving out the tomatoes. Add the seasonings and vinegar and then the tomatoes on top. Cover and simmer for another 25 minutes until bubbly. Can be served hot or cold.

Candied Sweet Potatoes

Serves 4

This recipe is simple and delicious, and you don't need an oven for it. Kids will eat it too!

2 large sweet potatoes, peeled and
    cut in half lengthwise

2–3 T honey
water

Place sweet potatoes in large frying pan with lid, and cover the bottom of the pan with about an inch of water. Cover the pan tightly and cook on low flame for 45 minutes, checking periodically that it doesn't burn. Add in honey about 10 minutes before the end of cooking time. Turn off flame and leave covered until it cools down. Serve warm.

Zucchini 'n Tomato Sauce

Serves 4–6

5 medium zucchini,
   scrubbed or peeled
1 medium onion, sliced
1 1/2 tsp. salt

1/2 tsp. pepper
2 T. olive oil
2/3 cup tomato sauce or 3–4 fresh red
   tomatoes, peeled and pureed.

Heat olive oil in bottom of pan and saute the onions until lightly browned. Slice zucchini and layer on top of onions, cover and let steam for 20 minutes. No water is necessary as zucchini emits a lot of water while it cooks. Add seasonings and tomato sauce. Simmer for another 35 minutes. Can be served hot or cold.

Squash and Vegetable Bonanza

Serves 4–6

1 large onion, sliced
4 large garlic cloves, sliced
2 medium zucchinis, scrubbed
   and cubed
1 butternut squash or large piece of
   pumpkin, peeled and cubed

1 red pepper, sliced thin
1 orange or yellow pepper, sliced thin
1/4 cup olive oil
1/4 tsp. pepper
3 sprigs rosemary or 1 tsp. dried
1/2 tsp. oregano

Toss all the ingredients together in a large bowl until well coated. Place into 9x13 inch baking pan. Cover loosely with silver foil. Bake at 350°F/180°C for 45 minutes. Remove from oven immediately.

SIDE DISHES & COOKED SALADS

Meat-Filled Squash

Serves 3–6

1 lb. / 500 grams ground meat
1 lb. / 500 grams ground turkey or
    chicken
2 eggs
1/2 tsp. pepper
1 large potato, peeled and grated
1 medium carrot, peeled and grated
1 large onion, diced and sautéed
2 cloves garlic, diced, optional
3 medium acorn squash *

Sauce:
2–3 cups tomato paste
2 cups water
3–4 tsp. salt to taste
3/4 tsp. pepper
2 T. lemon juice
1/2 cup brown sugar, optimal; if not,
    use white sugar

Wash the outside of the squash. In a large bowl, mix all the rest of
the ingredients, except for sauce. Slice off the narrow end of each
squash and clean out cavity. Stand the squash up on its wider end
and fill it with the meat mixture until it is 3/4 of the way full.

Mix the sauce ingredients. Spoon sauce generously on top of each
squash so that some of it will get absorbed and enter the cavity; then
pour all the rest of it into the pan. Bake covered for an hour on
350°F/180°C until squash is tender. Serve immediately.

Beet Latkes

Serves 4

3 cups of cooked and shredded beets,
drained
2 eggs, beaten
1/4 cup sugar

3/4 cup potato starch
1 T. lemon juice
1/8 tsp. salt

Mix all ingredients and fry on both sides in oil. Serve immediately.

Red Waldorf Salad

Serves 4

1 1/2 green apples, peeled and grated
2 cups cooked beets, shredded
1/2 cup chopped celery
1/2 cup walnuts, chopped

3 T. lemon juice
2 1/2 T. sugar
1 T. mayonnaise, optional

Mix all ingredients together and refrigerate.

Marinated Asparagus Spears

Serves 6

1 1/2 lbs./750 grams fresh
   asparagus spears, cleaned
   and checked
1/4 cup water

Marinade:
3/4 cup oil
1/4 cup white wine or apple cider
   vinegar
1 tsp. onion powder
1 tsp. garlic powder
1/4 tsp. pepper
1 tsp. basil
1 tsp. oregano
1 tsp. dried parsley flakes, optional
2 tsp. sugar, optional

Steam the spears with the water in a tightly covered pot until you
see steam; this should take just about 5 minutes. Turn off pot and
immediately drain the spears. They will still appear very uncooked;
this is fine. Place in a plastic container. Mix together the Marinade
(Italian Dressing) ingredients and shake well. Pour over spears in
the container, cover well, and let it sit overnight. Serve cold or at
room temperature.

Tip:
This marinade is
excellent also as
Italian Dressing, to
be served over fresh
salads. It keeps well
in the fridge for at
least 2 weeks.

Letcho

Serves 4–6

2 big onions, diced
1/2 lb. fresh mushrooms or 8 oz.
   canned, sliced
8 beef tomatoes, cubed
2 red peppers, sliced thin
1 green pepper, diced

4 big zucchinis, cubed
2 T. olive oil
1 tsp. salt
1/4 tsp. black pepper
 4 eggs

Sautee all vegetables in oil until soft. Add salt and pepper. Beat
eggs slightly with a fork and add to the vegetables. Stir and serve.

This may be served as a side dish as is, or with mashed potatoes or
Gefen Gluten-Free Noodles.

Tip:
To make a really
beautiful entrée out
of this, scoop out
the seeds of a whole
acorn squash and
fill the squash's cavi-
ty with this letcho.
Cover and bake for
an hour until soft.

Broccoli Stuffed Tomatoes   *Serves 4*

4 medium tomatoes, washed
1/4 tsp. salt
1/4 tsp. white pepper
1 T. oil

1/2 cup onion, diced
1 garlic clove, minced, optional
1 cup cooked chopped broccoli
1/2 tsp. lemon juice

Preheat oven to 350°F/180°C. Cut a thin slice from stem end of each tomato and finely dice these slices. Scoop out pulp from each tomato, leaving 1/4 inch thick shells. Chop pulp and set aside. Sprinkle salt and pepper evenly over inside of each tomato shell. Set shells upside down on paper towels and let drain. Saute onion and garlic in the oil until translucent, 3–5 minutes. Add reserved diced tomato and pulp. Reduce heat and cook, stirring occasionally until moisture has evaporated, about 10–15 minutes. Remove from heat and stir in broccoli, reserving 1/4 cup of florets. Spoon 1/4 of mixture into each shell and place upright in a 8x8x2 inch baking dish. Brush tomatoes with oil. Bake 20–30 minutes until tomatoes are soft and skins are just starting to split. Garnish with reserved broccoli florets.

Spicy Sweet Potatoes   *Serves 4–6*

4 large sweet potatoes
1 onion, sliced in rings
6 garlic cloves, peeled, left whole
5 T. olive oil

2–3 sprigs fresh rosemary or
    1 tsp. dried
1/4 tsp. pepper

Peel or scrub sweet potatoes and cube. Slice half the garlic cloves. In a large bowl, toss sweet potatoes with all the ingredients. Place in a pan lined with baking paper and bake covered for 45 minutes at 350°F/180°C To make them crispier, uncover for the last 10 minutes. Serve warm.

Sweet Potato Scoops

Serves 12–15

8 medium sweet potatoes
2 T. oil
12–15 pineapple rings

1 packet vanilla sugar
1/2 cup plus 2 T. brown sugar
1 tsp. cinnamon

Boil or bake sweet potatoes until soft. Mash up with the oil, 1/2 cup sugar, and vanilla sugar. Lay out the pineapple rings on a lined cookie sheet. Scoop the mixture with an ice cream scooper and place each scoop on top of a pineapple ring. Sprinkle with the 2 T. of brown sugar and cinnamon. Bake uncovered at 350°F/180°C for 45 minutes, until slightly crispy on top.

Tip:
For added garnish, 1 black raisin or 1 Craisin can be added to the top of each scoop, as seen featured in the photo here.

Yams 'n Oranges

Serves 4–6

4 yams or sweet potatoes, sliced
2 medium oranges, peeled and sliced
1/2 cup packed brown sugar or honey
1 cup fresh orange juice

3 T. oil
1 tsp. cinnamon
3/4 cup chopped walnuts
orange slices for garnish, optional

Place half of the yams in a greased casserole dish. Place half of the orange slices over this and sprinkle with 4 T. of the brown sugar or honey. Repeat with remaining halves. Combine orange juice and oil. Pour over all. Sprinkle with walnuts and cinnamon. Bake covered at 325°F/170°C for an hour, basting with the orange sauce occasionally. Serve warm, garnished with the additional orange slices.

Note:
See photograph on page 63

Stuffed Squash

Serves 4–6

2 squash, acorn or butternut
2 tsp. fresh lemon juice
1/2 cup raisins or Craisins
2 cups apples, cubed or shredded

4 T. slivered or chopped almonds
1 tsp. cinnamon
2 T. brown sugar
2 tsp. oil

Cut each squash in half lengthwise; remove seeds and any stringy parts. This is easier to do if you first bake the squash covered in the oven for about 30 minutes. Combine lemon juice, fruits, nuts, cinnamon, and brown sugar. Spoon this mixture into the cavity of each squash and drizzle oil over all. Place open side up in deep baking dish with one inch of water covering the bottom. Cover and bake at 375°F/190°C for an hour. Uncover for the last 15 minutes. If the squash was baked alone first, the baking time when stuffed is reduced. Serve alone or with mashed potatoes.

Homemade Pickles

Large glass jar, 2 quart/2 liters in size,
  with lid that closes securely
Bunch of small cucumbers,
  washed very well but not peeled
3 garlic cloves

large bunch fresh dill, or 1 T. dried
2 T. (wine) vinegar
2 T. pickling spices
water
salt

Make sure glass jar and lid are very clean. To sterilize, pour boiling water over them. Place a knife blade under jar when pouring water so it won't crack. Clean off garlic pieces, slice each in half, and place in jar. Add in the dill. Clean cucumbers well as directed. Pack them as tightly as possible into jar, stem side up for easier removal later.

Fill a large bowl with 4 cups of water. Add to it a little less than 1/4 cup regular or coarse salt and stir briskly until dissolved. This should be your ratio when preparing the saltwater. Place spices and vinegar into jar. Pour salt water over all, filling jar to top. Cover tightly and shake back and forth a few times to mix up the spices. Place on a sunny windowsill for two days until color starts to change, then in a cool, dark place for another 4–5 days. Underneath the sink is a great spot. For a half-sour taste, let them sit less time.

Hungarian Letcho   *Serves 4–6*

2 large onions, sliced in rings
4 large garlic cloves, diced
1 green pepper, sliced thin
1 red pepper, sliced thin
2 small tomatoes, peeled and cubed
2 medium-large zucchini, chopped
1 carrot, sliced in thin rounds,
  optional

3/4 cup water
4 T. tomato paste or 1 fresh tomato,
  peeled and pureed
1/4 tsp. cumin, optional
1/4 tsp. pepper
1/2 tsp. salt
1 T. paprika
1/4 cup olive oil

Saute the onions and garlic in a frying pan until soft, for about 5 minutes. Add in the rest of the vegetables. Add the remaining ingredients and simmer on low flame for about 45 minutes, until very soft. Serve hot.

NOTES TO REMEMBER

Potatoes &
More Potatoes

Shepherd's Pie, page 84

Spicy Baked Potatoes

Serves 6

8 large potatoes, peeled and cubed
1 onion, diced
4–6 garlic cloves, sliced

1/2 cup olive oil
1 T. paprika
1/2 tsp. pepper

Place potatoes, onion and garlic in large bowl and toss with oil and seasonings until very well coated. Line a 9x13 inch baking pan with baking paper and spread the contents in it. Bake covered at 350°F/180°C for 50 minutes, then uncover and bake 10 more minutes until tender and done. Serve immediately.

Fluffy Potato Puffs

Serves 4–6

10 medium-large potatoes,
    peeled and cut into chunks
1 large onion, diced, optional

2 T. oil
salt and pepper

Boil potatoes until very soft. Drain water and mash potatoes until smooth. If using onion, saute onion in a small amount of oil until brown and add to mashed potatoes. Add salt and pepper to taste. Cover large baking sheet with baking paper and spread a coating of oil over it. Form balls out of the potato mixture and lay them side by side on baking sheet. Bake at 350°F/180°C until they are golden brown and crunchy, about 30–45 minutes. Serve immediately.

Variation:
For those who do broch, or at least on the 8th day, the balls can be rolled in matza meal before being placed in pan.

Potato Chremslach

Serves 4–6

6 potatoes, cooked and mashed
4 eggs
1 1/2 tsp. salt

1/8 tsp. pepper
oil for frying

Combine the first flour ingredients. Heat oil in large frying pan. Drop the batter by tablespoons into hot oil and fry until medium brown on both sides. Serve hot.

Suggestion:
Can be served with applesauce or for dairy version, with sour cream.

Bubby's Potato Kugel

Serves 10–12

10 large potatoes, peeled
2 onions
7 eggs

2 tsp. salt
1 tsp. pepper
1/3 cup olive oil

Oven: Pour oil in a 9x13 inch pan and place in 375°F/190°C oven to preheat. Puree onions in food processor until liquid. Grate the potatoes into the onions. Empty into large bowl, without draining off liquid. Add eggs and spices to grated potatoes in bowl and mix well. Remove pan from oven and pour in kugel batter slowly and carefully as the oil can splatter. Bake at 375°F/190°C for 1 1/2 hours, covering loosely with foil if it starts to get too brown on top.

Stovetop: When frying up the kugel, either use two large frying pans or only make 1/2 the recipe at a time. It will not fit into one frying pan. Prepare kugel as instructed above, omitting the oil. Then heat up oil in a large frying pan. Pour in batter and cook about 1/2 hour until nicely browned on bottom, turn over, and fry on second side for another 20 minutes, or until done.

Reduced Fat and Cholesterol-Free Potato Kugel

Serves 8

8–9 large potatoes, peeled
2 large onions
8–9 egg whites

2 tsp. salt
1/2 tsp. pepper
1/4 cup olive oil

Pour oil in a 9x13 inch pan and place in 375°F/190°C oven to pre-heat. Place onions in food processor and puree until liquid. Change blades and grate the potatoes into the onions. Empty into large bowl, without draining off liquid. Add egg whites and spices to grated potatoes in bowl and mix well. Remove pan from oven and pour in kugel batter slowly and carefully. Bake for an hour, or until the kugel is brown and crispy on top.

Fleishig Potato Kugel

Serves 8–10

8–9 large potatoes, peeled
2 large onions
4 large garlic cloves, minced
1/4 cup oil

2 tsp. salt
1/2 tsp. pepper
paprika
2 1/4 lbs./1 kilo flanken, cut into chunks

Preheat oven to 375°F/190°C. Pour oil in a 9x13 inch pan and place in oven. Puree the potatoes, onions, and garlic together until smooth. Add salt and pepper. Remove pan carefully from oven and pour in half of the kugel mixture, very slowly, as oil is very hot. Add the chunks of meat on top, then spread the rest of the kugel over it. Sprinkle generously with paprika over the top. Bake for 1 1/2 hours, covering loosely with foil if it starts to get too brown on top.

Note:
This can be done quite successfully in a crock pot. The night before serving, prepare kugel the same way and let it cook on very low setting until next day.

Crispy Rosemary Potatoes

Serves 4–6

8 potatoes, peeled and cubed or
    3 lbs. unpeeled baby potatoes
1/2 cup olive oil
10 garlic cloves, peeled and quartered

4 sprigs fresh rosemary or 1 T. dried
1 tsp. onion powder
1/4 tsp. pepper

Combine all ingredients except rosemary sprigs in large bowl. Toss well to coat evenly. Layer in a 9x13 inch pan lined with baking paper. Place the rosemary sprigs all over and stuff down in between the mixture. Cover and bake at 400°F/200°C for an hour, stirring occasionally to brown more evenly. Uncover for the last 10 minutes. Serve immediately.

Shepherd's Pie

Serves 4–6

6 medium potatoes, peeled
1 lb./1/2 kilo ground meat,
   chicken or turkey
2 eggs or 3 egg whites
1 large onion, diced
1 box fresh mushrooms, sliced

1/2 cup cold water
1 tsp. salt
1/2 tsp. pepper
paprika to taste
olive oil

Prepare the meat mixture by placing meat in a bowl, and mixing it with eggs, onion, mushrooms, water, salt and pepper until well blended. Set aside. Grease all sides of casserole dish or small square pan. Grate potatoes and layer half on bottom of pan. Now layer meat mixture. Then add rest of the grated potatoes on top of the meat. Sprinkle top generously with paprika. Drizzle more oil all over top of pie. Let it bake uncovered at 350°F/180°C until potatoes on top are very done, about 45–65 minutes.

Potatoes 'n Garlic

Serves 6–8

4 potatoes, peeled and cubed
4 sweet potatoes, peeled and cubed
4 garlic cloves, peeled
4 T. oil
1 T. lemon juice

3 T. orange juice
1 tsp. thyme
1/2 tsp. dried parsley
1/2 tsp. dried dill

Bake the potatoes, sweet potatoes, and garlic covered in a 9x13 inch pan at 400°F/200°C for an hour until browned. Remove from oven. Remove garlic cloves to a bowl, and combine with the rest of the ingredients. Mash together and place inside pan. Place back in the oven for another 15 minutes. Right before serving, toss together well. Serve warm.

Potato Salad

Serves 4–6

6 potatoes, peeled and boiled
2 stalks celery, diced
1/2 green pepper, diced, optional
2 pickles, diced, optional
1 large carrot, grated
1 small onion, diced
1 scallion, diced

1–2 hard boiled eggwhites,
   diced, optional
2 tsp. (wine) vinegar, or 1 tsp. each
   vinegar and lemon juice
1 tsp. salt
1/2 tsp. paprika
1/4 tsp. pepper
1/3 cup mayonnaise

Dice boiled potatoes into a large bowl. Add in all the other vegetables and then the eggs. Sprinkle in spices and vinegar. Mix. Add mayonnaise to taste. Mix again and refrigerate.

Low Fat French Fries

Serves 6

6–8 large potatoes, peeled
2 T. olive oil

paprika and pepper to taste
onion powder to taste, optional

Preheat oven to 400°F/200°C. Slice potatoes into thin french fry size strips. Place in a large bowl and add the oil and spices. Toss to coat evenly. Spread out on large cookie sheet lined with parchment paper. Bake for 45 minutes to 1 hour, using a spatula to mix up the potatoes periodically so it will brown more evenly. Bake until crispy and golden brown. Serve hot. Kids just love this one!

NOTES TO REMEMBER

Dairy Delights

Mushroom Quiche, page 93

Broccoli and Cauliflower Bake

Broccoli and Cauliflower Bake   *Serves 4–6*

1/2 bag Bodek broccoli florets
1/2 bag Bodek cauliflower
2 medium onions, diced
2 medium zucchini, peeled and
*   sliced thin*
5 eggs or 7 egg whites

1 cup cottage cheese
1 cup shredded yellow cheese
1 tsp. salt
1/4 tsp. pepper
2 T. oil

Heat oil in frying pan and saute onions for 15 minutes until light brown. Layer in zucchini and then the broccoli and cauliflower. Cover and let steam for 10 minutes. Transfer everything to a large bowl. Add in the eggs, cottage cheese, and seasonings. Mix well and place half the mixture in a large casserole dish. Sprinkle with half the shredded cheese. Then pour in the rest of the mixture. Cover loosely with foil and bake for 45 minutes at 325°F/170°C. Uncover and sprinkle rest of cheese on top. Continue baking for another 15 minutes, until cheese is melted and bubbling. Serve immediately.

Zucchini Casserole   *Serves 4*

6 medium zucchini, sliced into 1/4
*   inch rounds*
1 large onion, sliced
1/2 cup cottage cheese
1/2 cup farmer cheese or 5% soft
*   white Israeli cheese*

1/2 cup shredded yellow cheese
1 tsp. salt
1/2 tsp. pepper
2 T. oil
1 cup canned mushrooms, optional

Saute onions in oil in frying pan for 10 minutes until browned. Add the zucchini to the onions, cover pan and let steam for 10 minutes. Transfer vegetables to a big bowl and mix in the mushrooms, seasonings, cottage cheese and white cheese. Pour half into a casserole dish, sprinkle on some yellow cheese and then pour in rest of mixture. Bake covered at 325°F/170°C for 45 minutes. Uncover and sprinkle with rest of shredded cheese. Bake another 15 minutes until cheese is melted. Serve immediately.

DAIRY DELIGHTS

Mexican Pepper Bake

Serves 6

6 peppers, 2 each of red, green,
    orange, or yellow, cut into strips
2 large onions, sliced
3 garlic cloves, diced
1 tsp. cumin
1 tsp. coriander (kuzbara)
1/4 tsp. black pepper
1 tsp. paprika
1/4 tsp. cayenne pepper
    (paprika charifa)

1 1/2 T. potato starch
2 T. cold water
1 1/2 cups cheddar, parmesan or
yellow cheese, sliced or shredded
2 T. oil

Topping Ingredients:
4 large eggs
1 1/2 cups sour cream,
    or 5% soft cheese

Saute peppers, onions, and garlic in the oil on a low flame until soft, about 15 minutes. Add in spices. In a separate bowl, mix the potato starch with the water and pour into the sauteed vegetables. Stir well. Cook a few more minutes until liquid is gone. Line an 8x10 inch pan with baking paper. Layer some of the pepper mixture on the bottom. Sprinkle the yellow cheese on top of peppers. Cover with last layer of peppers.

To prepare topping:

First beat the eggs and then mix in the sour cream. Pour this over the top of the layers and sprinkle more regular paprika over it. Bake for 45 minutes at 325°F/170°C covered. Uncover and bake another 15 minutes. Serve warm.

Spinach Casserole

Serves 4

1 bag Bodek spinach
1 onion, diced
3 eggs
2 potatoes, peeled
1 tsp. salt

1/2 tsp. pepper
1 cup milk or pareve milk
1/2 cup shredded yellow cheese
oil

Saute onion in oil. Boil potatoes and mash with milk. Mix all the ingredients together except the shredded cheese and bake covered in a small casserole dish for 45 minutes at 325°F/170°C. Uncover and sprinkle shredded cheese on top. Bake another 10 minutes. Serve hot.

Salad Nicoise

Serves 6

1 head iceberg or romaine lettuce,
   shredded
2 tomatoes, cubed
2 cucumbers, chopped
1/2 cup purple cabbage, shredded
2 hard boiled eggs, chopped
1 can tuna, drained

1/2 cup slivered almonds or coarsely
   chopped pecans or walnuts,
   optional
1/2 cup crumbly white cheese such as
   feta or salty cheese
olive rings and pickles, optional

For an added twist, you may like to try any of the following: mandarin orange slices, mango slices, or a handful of Craisins for added garnish and taste.

Divide the ingredients into six portions. In each bowl layer in this order: lettuce, cabbage, tomato, cucumber, olive rings and/or diced pickles. Then either on top or on the side of the vegetables, layer tuna and some chopped egg. Crumble some white cheese over all. For added garnish, sprinkle nuts on top of each portion. Serve with a choice of dressings in the center of the table.

Eggplant Parmesan

Serves 6–8

2–3 medium, firm eggplant
2 cups 5%–9% cottage cheese
2 cups mozzarella cheese, shredded
2 eggs
7 garlic cloves, minced
2 T. parsley flakes
oil

Sauce:
1 cup tomato sauce
2 T. olive oil
1/2 tsp. oregano
1/2 tsp. basil
1 T. onion powder
1 1/2 tsp. salt
1/2 tsp. pepper

Slice eggplant the long way. Soak in salt water for 15 minutes;
rinse and dry off. Lay out slices on cookie sheet, sprinkle some oil
on top and broil in oven until light brown. Set aside. Then prepare
ingredients for sauce. Preheat oven to 350°F/180°C. Grease the
bottom of a 9x13 inch pan, or line it with baking paper. Mix cottage cheese together with minced garlic, eggs, and parsely flakes.
Layer in the following order: eggplant, cottage cheese mix, mozzarella cheese, and sauce. Continue layering, ending with eggplant
and sauce on top. Save the last bit of mozzarella for later. Cover
pan and bake 1 1/4 hours. Uncover and layer with the last of the
mozzarella cheese. Bake 10 more minutes until cheese is bubbling.

Pizza Potatoes

Serves 4–6

6 potatoes
1/4 cup oil
1 cup tomato sauce, or 5–7 fresh
    tomatoes, peeled and pureed
1 tsp. oregano
1/2 tsp. basil

1/4 tsp. pepper
1 tsp. salt
1/2 tsp. parsley flakes, optional
2 T. oil
1 1/2 cups shredded yellow cheese
    of any kind

Peel potatoes and slice into 1/4 inch rounds. Line 9x13 inch pan
with baking paper. Pour 1/4 cup oil into pan and coat evenly. In a
bowl, mix together the tomato sauce with seasonings and 2 T. oil.
Layer half the potatoes in the pan and cover well with some sauce.
Sprinkle half the cheese on top. Repeat this order, ending with
sauce and cheese on top layer. Cover and bake for an hour at
350°F/180°C. Reduce heat and uncover "pizza". Bake another
15–20 minutes, watching that the cheese does not burn.

Mushroom Quiche

Serves 4

Note:
See photograph on
page 87.

1 cup canned or fresh mushrooms
2 large onions, sliced
1/4 tsp. nutmeg, optional
1/4 tsp. curry, optional
1/4 tsp. black pepper
1/2 tsp. salt

1 tsp. garlic powder
4 eggs
1 1/4 cups grated cheese of any kind
1 cup cottage cheese or cream cheese
2 T. oil

Saute onions in oil until light brown. Add in spices and the mushrooms and cook a few more minutes, stirring every few minutes. Beat eggs lightly and add to mushroom mixture. Add cottage cheese or cream cheese and half of grated cheese and mix well. Then pour into pie plate. Top with remaining cheese and bake uncovered at 350°F/180°C for 45 minutes, until light brown and firm.

Rumple Crumple (Layered Potatoes 'n Eggs)

Serves 6–8

6 potatoes, peeled
8 hard boiled eggs, sliced
8 oz. sour cream

5 T. butter
3 T. oil
salt

Slice potatoes and cook until almost soft. Place oil in a deep pot or pan. Place one layer of sliced potatoes on bottom. Dot with butter and sprinkle with salt. Place one layer of sliced eggs onto potatoes. Dot with butter and sprinkle with salt. Spread thin layer of sour cream over the eggs. Repeat layering with potatoes, eggs and sour cream, ending with potatoes. Dot butter and sprinkle with salt in between layers. Sprinkle salt on top. Cook over medium heat for 35 minutes or bake at 400°F/200°C for 45 minutes.

DAIRY DELIGHTS

NOTES TO REMEMBER

Cakes, Cookies, & More

Almond Torte, page 100

Almond Brittle

1 cup almonds or walnuts,
   coarsely chopped

1 1/2 cups sugar
small pinch of salt

Prepare a large piece of silver foil on countertop. Then heat sugar over a low-medium flame, stirring constantly with a wooden spoon, until it is completely melted. Quickly stir in nuts and salt and remove from flame. Spread mixture evenly on the silver foil as much as possible, before it begins to harden, using the wooden spoon to flatten it. Allow to cool. Break into chunks and store in tightly sealed container or plastic bag.

Banana Nut Cake

10 eggs, separated
1 1/4 cups sugar
3–4 ripe bananas

3/4 cup walnuts or pecans,
   coarsely ground
3/4 cup potato starch

Preheat oven to 350°F/180°C. Beat egg whites until stiff. Beat yolks together with everything else. Fold whites into yolks carefully until well blended. Pour batter into greased tube pan. Bake for 35–40 minutes, until edges start to spring away slightly from sides of pan. Remove from oven and let cool completely. Remove from pan. If it seems moist to you, let it sit open for an hour or so before you wrap it up.

Strawberry Meringue Pie

Serves 6–8

4 egg whites
1 heaping cup sugar
1 tsp. lemon juice

4 cups fresh strawberries, sliced
fruit-flavored liqueur

Preheat oven to 275°F/135°C. Beat egg whites until foamy. Gradually add sugar, beating well after each addition until sugar dissolves. Beat an additional 10 minutes on high, slowly adding the lemon juice. Spoon into lightly greased pie dish, building up the sides to form a pie shell. Turn down heat to 250°F/120°C and bake for 1 hour. Shut off heat, open oven door slightly and let the "pie shell" dry inside for another hour. Fill with fresh sliced strawberries lightly tossed with fruit liqueur.

White Coconut Chiffon Cake

6 eggs, separated
1 1/4 cup sugar
2 T. oil

3/4 cup potato starch
2 T. lemon juice
1 cup shredded coconut

Preheat oven to 350°F/180°C. Beat egg whites until stiff. Set aside. In a separate bowl, beat yolks with oil until thick, then add remaining ingredients. Fold the two mixtures together. Pour batter into a tube pan. Bake until lightly browned on top and springy to the touch, approximately 30–40 minutes. Check to ensure it does not burn.

Baking Tips:

✦ To ensure that potato starch will not be lumpy, use a very small hand sifter and sift the measured potato starch just before you put it into your recipe.

✦ One 3 oz. square of baking chocolate equals 2 T. cocoa plus 1 T. vegetable oil (or use Pesach chocolate!)

✦ 1 cup of confectionary sugar equals 1 cup of granulated sugar pulverized in the blender together with 1 tsp. potato starch sifted into it afterwards. Pulverize 1/4 cup of sugar at a time until you reach the desired amount.

Famous Brownies

6 eggs
2 2/3 cups sugar
1 1/2 cups potato starch
3/4 cup cocoa
3/4 cup oil
1 tsp. vanilla
1 cup walnuts, coarsely chopped
1/2 cup coconut, optional

Chocolate Glaze:
1 cup powdered sugar
2 T. oil
2 T. hot water
2 T. cocoa

Preheat oven to 350°F/180°C. Mix all ingredients together until well blended. Bake in lightly greased 9x13 inch baking pan for 20–30 minutes until cake tester comes out mostly clean when inserted in center of cake. Do not overbake as then it will be too dry. Let cake cool. Mix together the ingredients for chocolate glaze and spread over brownies. Let the frosting harden before cutting and serving.

Double Layer Fancy Yom Tov Cake

Make one recipe of the Famous Brownies on page 98, omitting the chocolate glaze, and one recipe of the White Coconut Chiffon Cake on page 97, in two tube pans. Set aside to cool. Then prepare the white frosting below:

White Frosting:
1 cup sugar
1/3 cup water
1 tsp. vanilla
1 tsp. vinegar
2 egg whites

Optional Glaze:
1/2 cup cocoa
1 1/2 cups sugar
1 cup water
2 tsp. vanilla

Melt sugar, water, vanilla, and vinegar together on stovetop. Cool. Beat egg whites and add the mixture to it while still beating. To assemble cake, place brownie cake on bottom as it is denser than the white cake. Frost on the sides and top. Then, place white cake on top of brownie cake and frost as well. Cake can be used this way or for added looks, make the optional chocolate glaze. Melt all of the ingredients together until dissolved. Drizzle the glaze from the center of the cake and down the sides.

Devil's Food Cake

1/2 cup cocoa
1 cup hot water or coffee
1 cup potato starch
1 tsp. baking soda
1/4 tsp. baking powder

1/2 cup oil
1 1/4 cups sugar
2 eggs
1 tsp. vanilla

Dissolve cocoa in hot liquid. Add vanilla. Set aside. Cream oil and sugar. Add in eggs and mix together. Alternately mix in liquid mixture and dry ingredients. Bake in 9x13 inch pan lined with parchment paper at 350°F/180°C for 35–45 minutes until done.

Tip:
This is a delicious recipe for a Pesachdik chocolate trifle.

Almond Torte

*Note:
For those who do not use margarine on Pesach, use recipe for chocolate glaze from Famous Brownies recipe on page 98.

two 8-inch round cake pans
1/2 cup potato starch
1 tsp. cocoa
1 1/2 cups blanched almonds, chopped
6 eggs, separated
1 cup sugar
1 T. dark rum, optional
1 tsp. vanilla

Chocolate Frosting and Filling:

3 eggs
9 T. sugar
3/4 cup semi-sweet chocolate pieces
3/4 cup margarine *
1 tsp. vanilla

Preheat oven to 350°F/180°C. Sift potato starch into large bowl and add cocoa. Mix in almonds and set aside. Beat yolks with 1/2 cup sugar until thick and pale yellow. Stir in rum and vanilla. Then beat egg whites until frothy, adding in the other 1/2 cup sugar gradually until stiff peaks form. Lightly pour in the yolk mixture on top of the whites and start to fold together by hand. Slowly add the starch/nut mixture to it as you are folding, spoonfuls at a time.

To prepare cake pans, measure their bottom circumference on two parchment sheets of baking paper. Trace and cut out from paper. Grease both pans well, then put cut-outs on bottom of pan, and grease the top of those as well. Spoon batter evenly into both pans. Bake for 25–30 minutes until cake tester comes out clean and the cake starts to move away from the sides of the pans. Let cool in pans for 5 minutes. Then invert on a rack to continue cooling and remove the baking paper.

To make the frosting:

In a double boiler, melt chocolate; add eggs and sugar and stir with a wire whisk until somewhat thickened. Remove from heat and beat in margarine and vanilla with an electric hand beater. Cover and let cool for an hour to set. Place one cake on a plate and frost the top and sides. Layer second cake and frost the top and sides. Sprinkle ground almonds on top of cake to decorate. Garnish with chocolate shavings if desired.

Strawberry Shortcake

8 eggs, separated
1 1/2 cups sugar
1 cup potato starch
1 T. vanilla sugar
juice of one lemon, or 2 T. orange
    juice and 1 T. lemon juice

Strawberry Sauce:
1lb./1/2 kilo fresh strawberries
2 T. lemon juice
1 cup sugar
1 T. potato starch
2 T. cold water

Preheat oven to 350°F/180°C. Beat egg whites until stiff, while slowly adding half the sugar. Beat yolks separately with the rest of sugar; add in remaining ingredients. Fold in whites. Bake in tube pan for 45–60 minutes until browned on top. Remove from oven and cool. To prepare sauce, clean and puree strawberries. Boil together sugar, lemon juice and strawberries. After it has cooled for 20 minutes mix together the 2 T. water and potato starch until smooth and add to the hot sauce. Stir until it thickens for about 2 minutes. Turn off heat. Immediately before serving, add sliced fresh strawberries on top of cake. Then pour sauce over all.

Suggestion: Cake can be garnished with freshly sliced strawberries and whip. Recipe for Whipped Topping can be found on page 108.

Suggestion: Strawberry sauce can be used as a topping on other cakes and ice creams.

Suggestion: Serve this together with a scoop of vanilla ice cream on top of the cake slices. Delicious and attractive!

Lemon Meringue Pie   *Serves 6–8*

4 eggs, separated
1 1/4 cups sugar
1 T. potato starch
dash salt

2 T. water
2 tsp. grated lemon rind
6 T. lemon juice

Make the cake from the above strawberry shortcake recipe and press down into a 9 inch pie plate. Mix yolks with 1/2 cup sugar in a saucepan. Add in potato starch, salt, water, rind, and juice and cook over low flame, stirring constantly, until thick and smooth. Remove from heat and cool. Beat whites until frothy, add rest of sugar and beat until stiff. Fold only half of the whites into the yolk mixture. Pour into waiting "pie shell." Cover with other half of whites and bake at 325°F/170°C for 15–20 minutes, until the meringue is light golden brown. Refrigerate until serving. Freezes well.

Mrs. Shachter's Mousse Rolls

10 eggs, separated
1 1/2 cups sugar or 2 cups
powdered sugar

3 T. potato starch
6 T. cocoa
2 T. vanilla

Beat egg whites and set aside. Beat yolks with sugar until thick. Add the remaining ingredients. Fold in whites. Then take out two kitchen towels, run them under water, and wring them out as much as possible. Lay them out on the counter in preparation for the cake rolls. Line two jelly roll pans with greased parchment paper. Divide the batter into the pans and bake at 375°F/190°C for 15 minutes. Insert toothpick in middle of cake to see if done. Remove pans from oven. Quickly and carefully flip cake out onto the waiting towels. Peel off wax paper slowly, and roll up the cake in the towel jelly roll style. Let cool for 30 minutes in this position.

To make filling, prepare one recipe of Mom's Famous Chocolate Mousse on page 115 and refrigerate until firm. To fill cakes, prepare two large sheets of silver foil, one per roll. Place a large piece of saran wrap on top of the foil. Unroll the cake rolls directly onto this (see 1,2). Spread mousse out over both cakes and roll back up with the help of the saran wrap (see 3,4,5). Gently cover with the foil. Freeze on cookie sheet until hard (see 6).

After cake rolls have hardened they can be frosted. Use either the glaze from the brownie cake recipe found on page 98, or melt 4 oz./100 grams parve chocolate together with 2 T. oil, stirring well. Spread glaze over rolls and allow to set (see 7). For added elegance, grated chocolate, ground nuts, coconut, or powdered sugar can be sprinkled on top of the frosted rolls according to your taste (see 8).

103

Nut Sponge Cake

6 large eggs, separated
3/4 cup sugar
3/4 cup ground hazelnuts or almonds
2 T. lemon juice
6–8 T. potato starch,
    sifted into the recipe

Strawberry Sauce:
1 cup strawberries
4 T. sugar
1–2 T. water
2 tsp. potato starch

White Sauce:
2 tsp. potato starch
2 T. vanilla sugar
2 small eggs
1 1/4 cups milk or water

Preheat oven to 350°F/180°C. Beat yolks with sugar until pale yellow and thick. Add lemon juice and mix again. In a separate bowl, beat whites until stiff. Fold in half the whites with the yolk mixture, carefully adding the nuts a bit at a time until all folded in. Fold in rest of whites. Sift in potato starch and fold again. Lightly grease a tube pan or 10 inch cake pan and pour in batter. Bake for 30–40 minutes until center is done. Let it cool, then remove from pan.

For a more elegant presentational look, cake can be served with the two sauces offered. Prepare strawberry sauce by boiling the berries and sugar gently over low heat about 10–15 minutes, just until the strawberries get soft. Liquify starch in water and blend with berries until smooth.Cook for another 5 minutes and remove from heat. To prepare white sauce, mix starch, sugar and eggs into a pasty mixture. Add the liquid. Bring to a boil over low flame, stirring constantly. Turn off before it is too thick. Allow to cool. To serve in a very special way, spoon a small amount of white sauce on each plate. Drizzle some of the strawberry sauce in its center, and then lay a wedge of cake off to its side, with a fresh strawberry on top for decoration.

Cheesecake

7 eggs, separated
2 cups sugar
2 1/2 lbs. farmer cheese
8 oz. cream cheese
16 oz. sour cream

2 T. vanilla extract
3/4 cup orange juice
3 T. potato starch
3 cups crushed ladyfinger cookies
5 T. butter, melted

Mix 2 cups of the crushed cookies evenly with melted butter and press into bottom of a 9x13 inch baking pan. Beat egg whites until foamy. Then add sugar and continue beating until stiff. Slowly add in the yolks along with the remaining ingredients except the potato starch. Mix well and then add potato starch. Pour batter over the crust in baking pan. Sprinkle rest of cookie mixture over the top. Bake at 350°F/180°C for an hour. Leave cake in oven to cool after turning off the heat to avoid cracking.

Chocolate Sponge Cake

10 eggs, separated
1 1/2 cups sugar

6 T. cocoa
3 T. potato starch

Preheat oven to 350°F/180°C. Beat whites until stiff, then add half the sugar while continuing to beat.Set aside. In another bowl, beat yolks with the rest of sugar until thick. Add remaining ingredients, beating until blended. Fold both mixtures together. While folding, if batter seems too liquidy, sift in a bit more potato starch. Bake in lightly greased tube pan for about 1 1/4 hours, checking after 50 minutes on its progress. Remove cake from oven and allow to cool for 15–20 minutes. Then flip it out onto a waiting piece of foil lined with paper towels. Wrap up gently. Freezes well.

Double Chocolate Meringue Kisses

1 ounce unsweetened chocolate

3 T. cocoa

3 T. plus 1 tsp. potato starch

1/2 tsp. instant coffee

3 large egg whites

3/4 cup sugar

1/3 cup chocolate chips

Preheat oven to 325°F/170°C. Chop square chocolate into small pieces. Place in food processor fitted with sharp "S" blade, together with cocoa. Grind finely. Add potato starch and process one more minute. In a bowl, mix the unbeaten egg whites and coffee. Let stand for 5 minutes and then beat until stiff peaks form. Add sugar 1 tablespoon at a time while you are beating. Continue beating for 6–7 minutes. Fold chocolate mixture into the whites, then fold in chocolate chips. Drop by teaspoonfuls 2 inches apart onto baking paper. Bake for 15–18 minutes until firm.

Chocolate Crinkle Cookies

2 cups potato starch

3/4 cup oil

3/4 cup cocoa

2 cups sugar

4 eggs

2 tsp. vanilla

2 tsp. baking powder

2 cups powdered sugar for rolling balls

Tip:
When placing balls on paper, space widely apart as the cookies spread out while baking and are delicate to handle.

Mix oil, cocoa, and sugar. Beat in eggs, one at a time. Add vanilla. Add in dry ingredients and chill batter several hours or overnight covered in refrigerator. After batter has been chilled, you may need to add more starch if it looks liquidy. Preheat oven to 350°F/180°C. Cover your hands well with powdered sugar and roll some batter into a ball. Make sure ball is coated completely in white. Bake on parchment paper for 10–15 minutes until just starting to crinkle. Freezes well.

Almond Meringue Cookies

1 cup ground unblanched almonds
3/4 cup sugar
1 T. potato starch

3 egg whites
1/4 tsp. almond extract, optional
24 blanched almond halves

Preheat oven to 300°F/150°C. Line two cookie sheets with baking paper. Mix together ground almonds and potato starch until well blended. Set aside. Beat the egg whites until stiff; add sugar gradually. Fold in remaining ingredients by hand. Drop by teaspoonfuls two inches apart on cookie sheets and press an almond half into the center of each one. Bake for 25 minutes or until very lightly browned. Remove from oven and place the whole sheet with cookies on it carefully onto a flat surface without removing the cookies. Let sit for 5 minutes then carefully lift off with a spatula and cool. Store in a tightly covered container. Freezes well.

Pictured:
Double Chocolate Meringue Kisses

Chocolate Crinkle Cookies

Almond Meringue Cookies

Hazelnut Cookies

Yields approximately 25

2 cups hazelnuts, toasted*
   and coarsely chopped
9 egg whites
1 cup plus 3 T. sugar

1 packet vanilla sugar
1 1/2 cups chocolate bits,
   coarsely chopped

Preheat oven to 325°F/170°C. Beat whites until stiff, gradually adding sugars. Turn off mixer and fold in nuts by hand. Pour mixture into saucepan and cook over low flame for 15 minutes until it thickens slightly. Let cool. Then add chocolate bits. Drop this mixture by half tablespoonsful onto cookie sheet lined with baking paper. Bake for 25–30 minutes.

*Tip:
To toast nuts, layer in a flat baking pan in an oven preheated to 300°F/150°C for 10 minutes. The peels will fall off of them afterwards.

Raisin Treats

4 oz./100 grams dark or light raisins
1/3 cup semi-sweet or sweet red wine

8 oz./200 grams pareve chocolate
1 T. oil

Place raisins in a flat plastic container and let them soak overnight in the red wine. The next day, drain raisins and dry on paper towels. Then melt chocolate over low flame, and add oil. Turn off flame and mix raisins into melted chocolate. Spoon out into small cupcake holders. Refrigerate or freeze until hardened.

Whipped Topping

1 cup vanilla sugar, finely blended
1 egg white

1 large apple, grated

Beat egg white until foamy. Gradually add sugar, beating constantly. Add apple and continue to beat until consistency of whipped cream.

Note:
This recipe makes enough to frost a 10-inch cake.

Apple Muffins

Yields 15–20

4 cups green apples, peeled
and diced
1 cup sugar
2 large eggs, beaten
1/2 cup oil
2 tsp. vanilla

1 1/4 cups potato starch
2 tsp. baking soda
2 tsp. cinnamon
1 cup white raisins, optional
1 cup chopped walnuts

*Tip:
Greasing the top of
the muffin tray pre-
vents the muffins
from sticking to the
top while baking,
thereby allowing
easier removal from
pan.

Preheat oven to 325°F/170°C. Mix together sugar and cinnamon
and toss with apples. Set aside. Beat eggs with oil and vanilla by
hand in a large bowl. Combine dry ingredients in a separate bowl.
Set aside. Add apples to the egg mixture. Stir in the dry ingredients mixture by spoonfuls until well combined. Mix in raisins and
walnuts at the end. Line muffin trays with muffin holders. Fill each
cup with batter almost until the top. Bake 25–30 minutes until
tester in center comes out clean and muffins are light brown on
top. Muffins fall slightly after they cool down. Freezes well.

Desserts & Drinks

Creamsicle Roll, page 116

Lemon Ice Cream

6–7 eggs, separated   1 tsp. grated lemon peel
1 cup sugar   1 tsp. vanilla
1/2 cup oil   1/2 cup coconut, optional

Beat egg whites until stiff; gradually add in sugar. Beat yolks
together with oil until thick, then add in lemon peel and vanilla.
Fold both mixtures together and sprinkle in coconut. Freeze.

Easy Vanilla Ice Cream

8–9 eggs, separated   1/2 cup oil
1 cup sugar   1 package or 3 tsp. vanilla sugar

Beat egg whites until stiff; gradually add in sugar. Turn down the
speed on mixer somewhat and continue beating in yolks, then the
oil and vanilla sugar. Place in large container and freeze overnight
before serving. For a chocolate swirl throughout the ice cream,
place 1/3 of cream into container and drizzle syrup over it.
Continue layering cream and syrup, ending with syrup on top.
Freeze immediately.

Variation:
For Vanilla
Chocolate Chip
Ice Cream:
Place ice cream into
foil pan or contain-
er. Grate some
chocolate into small
pieces. Sprinkle
over ice cream on
the top. Do not mix
in. It will sink in a
bit as it freezes.

For Vanilla
Chocolate Swirl:
Pour half of the
batter into pan.
Swirl chocolate
syrup liberally.
Layer the rest of the
batter with more
chocolate syrup and
freeze.

Fluffy Strawberry Ice Cream

6 eggs, separated   3/4 cup fresh strawberries, pureed
1 cup sugar   1 package vanilla sugar
1/2 cup oil

Puree strawberries and set aside. Beat eggs whites until stiff; gradually add sugar. In separate bowl, beat yolks with oil until thick,
adding vanilla sugar and pureed strawberries while continuing to
beat. Fold mixtures together and freeze.

Variation:
Add one ripe
banana to the
strawberries when
pureeing, for a
strawberry-banana
flavor instead.

Chocolate Coffee Ice Cream

6–7 eggs, separated
1 cup sugar
1/2 cup oil
2 tsp. cocoa

1 tsp. instant coffee
1 tsp. vanilla
3 T. chocolate pieces

Beat egg whites until stiff, gradually add in sugar. Set aside. In a separate bowl, beat yolks together with oil until thick, then add in remaining ingredients. Gently fold the two mixtures together. Freeze.

Coconut Chocolate Chip Ice Cream

Variation:
1/2 cup finely chopped walnuts can be added to yolk mixture for a nutty flavor.

6 eggs, separated
3/4 cup sugar
1/2 cup oil

2 tsp. vanilla
4 oz./100 grams shredded coconut
4 oz./100 grams grated chocolate

Beat egg whites until stiff, gradually add sugar. In a separate bowl, beat yolks with oil until thick, then add remaining ingredients. Fold mixtures together and freeze.

Strawberry Mousse   *Serves 6*

1 pint/450 grams fresh strawberries
1 T. orange marmalade or apricot
preserves
1 T. unflavored jello

1/4 cup fresh orange juice
3 T. orange-flavored liqueur
3 egg whites
3 T. sugar

Puree strawberries and stir in preserves. Dissolve jello in orange juice and combine with the pureed strawberries. Heat this mixture and stir until smooth. Cool, then add liqueur. Chill and stir occasionally until the mixture begins to thicken. Beat egg whites until foamy. Gradually beat in sugar to form stiff peaks. Fold the beaten whites into the chilled strawberry mixture and spoon into a plastic container or 4-cup mold, chilling until mixture is set.

Mom's Famous Chocolate Mousse   *Yields 6-8 servings*

8 eggs, separated
8 oz. semi-sweet chocolate
1 T. instant coffee

1/4 cup boiling water
2/3 cup sugar
1 tsp. vanilla

Beat egg whites until very stiff. Set aside. Melt chocolate. Dissolve coffee in the water. Stir in hot coffee to melted chocolate. In separate bowl, beat yolks until thick. Add sugar to the yolks gradually while beating. Add chocolate mixture and vanilla to yolks. Fold yolk mixture together with whites.

There are several options for what you can now do with this mousse:

✦ Freeze it and serve as a dark chocolate ice cream. Remove from freezer 5–10 minutes before serving. Can be topped with whipped cream.

✦ Place half of mixture in pie pan and bake at 350°F/180°C for 10–15 minutes making sure it does not burn. Remove from heat and let cool. Place other half of mixture in refrigerator while it is baking and cooling. After it has cooled, pour the refrigerated mousse over the baked part. Freeze. Add grated chocolate to top of pie for added decoration. Slice and serve while still frozen.

✦ Buy chocolate cups. Place a nice amount of mousse in each cup and refrigerate. Make this the same day you want to serve it. Can be topped with whipped cream or fresh berries of any kind.

✦ Crumble a brownie cake by hand and press crumbs down into a long, flat container or a pan somewhat smaller than a 9x13 inch. Pour the mousse on top of it and freeze. Cut into squares and serve garnished with a fresh strawberry in the middle of each square. For added elegance, first spoon some strawberry sauce on a plate, then place brownie square in sauce.

✦ Use as a filling for jelly roll cake (recipe on page 102).

Notes:
Recipe for
Whipped Topping
can be found
on page 108.

Recipe for
Famous Brownies
can be found
on page 98.

Recipe for
Strawberry Sauce
can be found
on page 104.

Creamsicle Roll
Yields 14 slices

Note:
See recipe and
instructions for
Strawberry Sauce
on page 104.

1 jelly roll pan lined with baking paper
1 flavor of jello sherbet from
Rainbow Sherbet on page 120
1 recipe of Easy Vanilla Ice Cream
on page 113

Make the sherbet part of this recipe first by choosing only one flavor of jello and following directions for it from the Rainbow Sherbet recipe. After it is beaten into a sherbet consistency, spread it out on a jelly roll pan lined with baking paper and freeze flat until solid (**see 1,2**). Then make the Easy Vanilla Ice Cream recipe. Only half the recipe amount is needed for one creamsicle roll. Pour the remainder of the ice cream batter into a container for freezing, or make two creamsicle rolls in one day. Spread the ice cream evenly on top of the sherbet layer and freeze until very solid, or overnight. Remove from freezer. Lift the whole thing out of the jelly roll pan onto a flat surface by holding onto the baking paper (**see 3**). If the creamsicle is too hard to work with, allow it to sit for 10 minutes before attempting to roll. Roll up like a jelly roll using the paper for help, pulling the paper away as you are rolling (**see 4,5,6,7**). Refreeze the roll immediately until hard again, then wrap it until ready to serve. Slice and serve with strawberry sauce on a plate (**see 8 and below**).

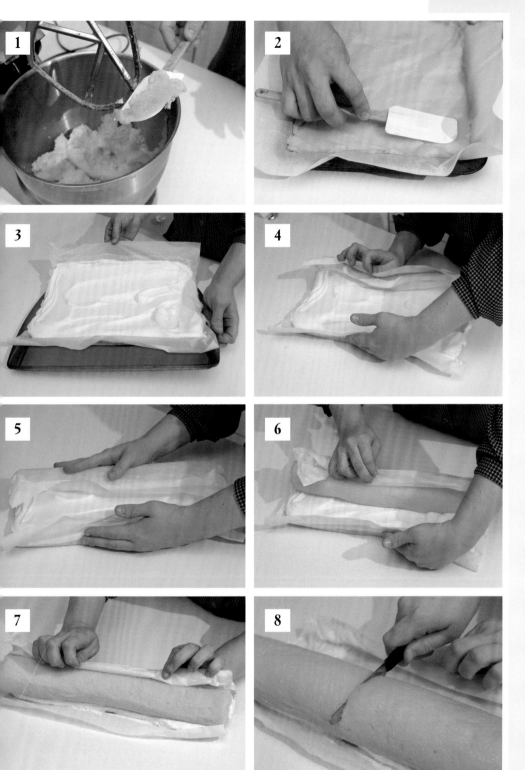

DESSERTS & DRINKS

Strawberry Orange Ices

6 cups/1.5 kilo fresh strawberries
1 3/4 cups fresh orange juice
1 3/4 cups sugar

1/2 cup freshly squeezed lemon juice
1/8 tsp. salt

Puree all ingredients together until smooth, doing a small amount at a time if necessary. Pour into 9x13 inch foil pan and freeze until firm, or overnight. Take out and let soften just enough to rebeat, then beat again with mixer until it looks like the consistency of sherbet. This step is very important because without it, the ices are just like a rock, instead of like sherbet. Refreeze. Take out of freezer about 10 minutes before serving for easier scooping.

Strawberry Snow   *Serves 6*

1/2 lb./250 grams fresh strawberries
1/2 cup sugar
1/8 tsp. lemon juice
1 egg white

Puree strawberries, adding sugar and lemon juice to them. Beat egg white until it starts to get foamy and white. While mixer is still beating, pour in strawberry mixture a bit at a time. You will find that the egg white will expand as you add the mixture to it. Then beat for 10–15 minutes. Freeze immediately when done. You can make this recipe with just about any fruit you want, such as banana, peach, apple, lemon, orange, etc. Just puree them as the strawberries, and continue as directed.

Orange Sherbet

Serves 4

1/2 tsp. jello
1/4 cup sugar
1 cup water

1/2 tsp. orange liqueur
6 oz. orange juice concentrate*
1 egg white

In a bowl, dissolve jello with a little cold water and stir. In a small saucepan, liquify sugar in the cup of water slowly over low heat and bring the mixture almost to the boiling point. Turn off heat. Add the softened jello to the sugar syrup as soon as it is removed from heat. Stir until all the jello is dissolved. Cool. Add orange juice concentrate and orange liqueur; stir well. Freeze for 1–2 hours. Beat egg white until stiff. Remove mixture from freezer and scoop out into bowl. Break up the frozen mixture with a fork until it is mushy, then fold together with the beaten egg white. Place the sherbet into container and return to freezer until firm, about 4–8 hours. Take out and let soften just enough to rebeat, then beat again with mixer until it looks like the consistency of sherbet. Refreeze until serving.

*Note:
To make your own "concentrate", squeeze about 10 juicy, sweet oranges, until you get 3/4–1 cup worth of juice, and freeze. Use this in place of the bought concentrated version.

Rainbow Sherbert

Variation:
If only working
with 2 colors, layer
the colors
i.e., red, yellow,
red, yellow

4 packages of different color jello   *2 cups sugar*
8 cups orange juice   *4 cups water*

The day before assembling, prepare the sherbet layers. Take 1 cup water and 1/2 cup sugar and boil them together. Add 1 package of jello and mix. Immediately add 2 cups orange juice to it and mix well. Place in freezer in a flat plastic container to freeze overnight. Repeat instructions with remaining jello packages. There should be 4 separate containers in the freezer.

The next day, remove one container of frozen jello from freezer and allow to soften for 10 minutes or so. Then beat with mixer until it is the consistency of sherbet (see 1). Spread sherbet in a 9x13 inch foil pan and place pan in freezer (see 2, 3, 4). About 1/2 hour later, when that layer has rehardened somewhat, do the same to a different color of jello, then spread this second layer on top of the first and refreeze again. Continue this way until you have all four layers in the pan (see 5). Cover with plastic wrap first and then foil, making sure to seal pan well. Freeze overnight before serving. Serve either cut in rectangular pieces or scooped in a dessert dish (see 6, 7, 8).

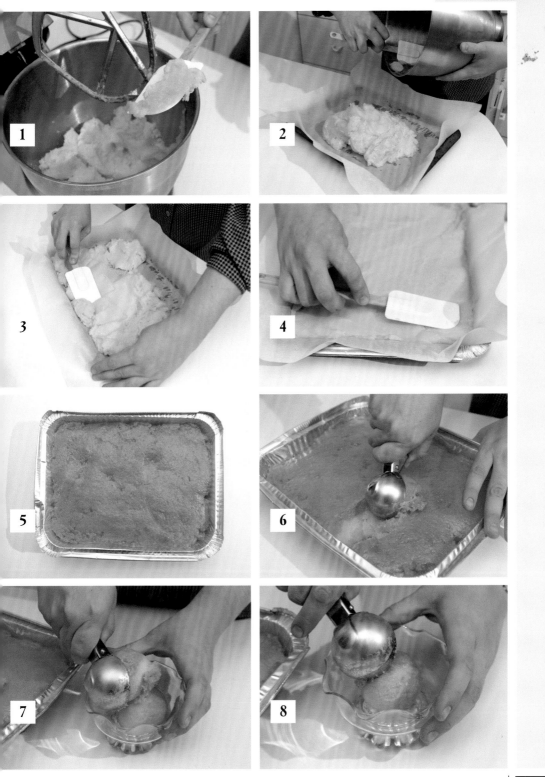

Rhubarb Ices

Serves 10

2 pints/500 grams fresh strawberries,
    hulled and cleaned
2 lbs./900 grams–1 kilo rhubarb,
    cleaned and chopped
2 cups semi-dry good quality
    white wine

2 1/2 cups sugar
1 1/2 T. fruit-flavored liqueur
1/2 cup freshly squeezed orange juice,
    pulp removed, optional

Place all ingredients in a large pot and cook covered over a low flame until soft, about 25–35 minutes. Turn off flame and puree until smooth. Pour into a large 9x13 inch pan and freeze for 4–6 hours, until mostly solid but not rock hard. If it becomes rock hard, let it defrost 20 minutes first before the next step.

Scoop frozen mixture into a mixing bowl and beat with a metal "K-hook" beater (NOT your egg beaters!) on medium speed until it resembles sherbet consistency. Refreeze until serving. Remove from freezer 10 minutes before serving for easier scooping.

Mousse Ice Cream Roll

Yields 30 servings (2 rolls)

Variation:
For added crunch, you may use shredded coconut, chopped walnuts, chocolate chips, or sprinkles. Simply line a flat surface and sprinkle your choice of crunch onto it, and roll the finished mousse roll in it until covered. Then refreeze.

Mousse Layer:	**Ice Cream Layer:**	
8 eggs, separated	8 eggs, separated	3 tsp. vanilla
11 oz./300 grams bitter-sweet chocolate	1/3 cup oil	1 package vanilla pudding
	1/2 cup sugar	
4 T. sugar	3/4 cup orange juice	

Mousse: Beat whites until stiff, adding sugar slowly. Set aside. Melt chocolate in double boiler. Beat yolks until thick, adding the melted chocolate to them. Fold in whites and divide evenly between two lined jelly roll pans. Freeze until solid; then do the ice cream layer.

Ice Cream: Beat whites until stiff; gradually add in sugar. Keep the mixer running, and add in vanilla, pudding, and juice. In separate bowl, beat yolks until thick while slowly adding oil. Fold mixtures together by hand, and divide evenly over the two pans of frozen mousse layers. Freeze again. Using the paper, roll up like a jelly roll (see page 117). Refreeze immediately.

Cocoa Blintze Pie

Serves 8–10

Blintze:	**Cocoa Filling:**
8 eggs	*1 cup cocoa*
1/8 tsp. salt	*2 cups sugar*
2/3 cup water	*1 cup ground walnuts*
1/2 cup potato starch	
oil	

Dissolve potato starch in water. In another bowl, beat eggs with salt. Then add the potato starch and water. Heat oil in frying pan. Drop 3–4 tablespoons of batter into pan, rotating pan to spread quickly to all sides. When lightly golden, flip blintze over and heat for another minute. Turn out onto plate. Continue this way until batter is used up. Then prepare cocoa filling by mixing all ingredients together. Layer blintzes with 2 tablespoons of filling in between each layer on an oven safe plate that fits into a 9x13 inch pan. Wrap up the pie in silver foil very well. Fill a 9x13 inch pan with 1 cup water. Place the plate inside the pan. Make sure the water does not reach the pie. Cover the pan with more silver foil and bake at 350°F/180°C for 30–45 minutes.

Heimishe Chocolate Schnapps

5 cups /1 kilo sugar	*1 T. coffee*
4 cups water	*4 oz./100 grams semi-sweet chocolate*
6 T. cocoa	*1 1/2 cups 90 proof alcohol*

Bring to a boil all the ingredients except the chocolate. When boiled, add chocolate and turn off heat. Stir together until chocolate is melted. Blend with an immersion blender until smooth, transferring it to a big bowl. Add the alcohol, Using a funnel, pour into clean glass bottles until about 3/4 full. Let sit overnight or several days. Shake well before drinking to lessen thickness. If it becomes too thick to pour, add a few drops of water to the bottle and shake vigorously. Makes about 2 1/2 wine bottles' worth of schnapps. Do not refrigerate.

Tip:
If the schnapps hardens in the bottle, simply add a few drops of water to the top of the bottle. Close and shake vigorously. Alternatively, run the bottle under hot water for a minute and shake.

Spiked Strawberry Drink

Serves 8–10

4 cups/1 kilo fresh strawberries
1 cup sugar
4 T. fresh lemon juice

1 cup semi-dry white wine
1 orange, peeled and pitted
3 cups water

Put all ingredients except water through blender, doing half at a time if necessary. Puree until very liquidy. Place in a big bowl and add the water. Using a funnel, pour into glass jars and refrigerate. It may have a strong alcohol taste at first but after sitting in the refrigerator it will mellow out. Serve chilled in wine glasses with a piece of cake on the side.

Iced Tea Sense

16 tea bags
boiling water
1 cup lemon juice

3 cups sugar
water

Pour some boiling water over the tea bags and let them soak for 5 minutes. Add lemon juice and sugar to the hot mixture. Then add enough plain water to make about 2 quarts of tea. Refrigerate. To serve, pour into pitcher and add ice cubes.

Yellow Russian (Eggnog)

1 1/2 cups water
1 cup sugar
7 egg yolks

1 package instant vanilla
pudding mix
3/4 cup 90 proof alcohol

Boil water with sugar. Allow to cool. Beat egg yolks well and add the other ingredients. Add to water mixture. Mix well. Makes a little more than one liter. No refrigeration necessary.

Fruity Punch

1 large bottle of strawberry fruit drink
1 large bottle of orange fruit drink, or
   2.5 quarts orange juice
2.5 quarts /2 liters apple or
cranberry juice
1 large bottle of soda water

1 cup sweet white wine or
   sparkling wine
several scoops of any flavor sherbet
ice cubes

Make this recipe right before serving. Pour all the liquid ingredients into a very large punch bowl. Add the ice cubes and then the sherbet so it will float on top of the liquid. Place punch bowl on table with ladle, or spoon into wine glasses with a piece of sliced orange or pineapple hanging off side of glass for decoration.

Chateau

1 1/2 cups of white wine
2/3 cup sugar
8 egg yolks

Boil wine and sugar in a pot. Allow to cool. Add egg yolks, beating vigorously. Reheat mixture until it boils, beating continuously until smooth and foamy. After boiling, remove from heat and beat a little longer. Serve immediately while it is still foamy. Serve either in a champagne glass or spooned over a slice of cake.

NOTES TO REMEMBER

Fresh Fruity Ideas

Crepe With Fruit and Ice Cream, page 131

Crepe with Fruit and Ice Cream

Yields 6 crepes

Note:
See photograph on page 129

10 T. potato starch
1/8 tsp. salt
2 eggs
1 cup orange juice
1/3 cup cold water
oil for frying

sliced fresh fruit for garnish such as
  any type of berries, strawberries,
  peaches, or melon slices
1 recipe of Easy Vanilla Ice Cream
  (page 113)

Sift the potato starch and salt into a bowl. Set aside. In another bowl, beat together the eggs, juice and water. Gradually add in starch mixture to the eggs, beating until smooth. Chill for at least half an hour. Remove from the refrigerator and remix for a few seconds with a spoon if it has separated.

Heat some oil in a frying pan, or use a non-stick pan. When oil is hot, pour in some batter, and rotating the pan, spread the batter evenly around the bottom of it. Fry for a few seconds until the edges start to curl and the center has several bubbles. Flip with spatula onto other side. Fry another minute until light brown. Slide off onto a plate. Continue until all the batter is used up. To serve, place a folded crepe on a plate. Arrange some of the sliced fruit on the side and a scoop of vanilla ice cream in the center.

Poached Pears

8–10 medium pears, peeled
1 package red jello
1/2 cup sugar

1/4 cup semi-dry red wine
water
1/2 tsp. cinnamon

In the bottom of a pot, place the pears standing up, packed as closely as possible. Add in the wine, sugar, jello, and cinnamon. Cover pears halfway with water. Boil over a low flame until pears are soft, about 35 minutes. Chill before serving. These are very pretty to serve as they become a soft pink color on the outside while retaining their white color on the inside.

Laced Citrus Salad

Serves 6–8

Choose a variety of citrus fruits such as pink or white grapefruits, pomelo, or oranges, and a variety of dried fruit such as dates, raisins, or Craisins.

Dressing:
1/3 cup sweet red wine
1/4 cup sugar
1–2 tsp. cinnamon
1/2 tsp. ginger, optional

Dice up citrus fruit into a bowl. Slice dried fruit and add in. Combine ingredients for dressing and pour over fruit. Let it marinate for several hours. When ready to serve, slice up an orange or grapefruit, unpeeled, into rings. Lay one ring on a plate, spoon some of the laced salad on top of it, and sprinkle shredded coconut over all.

Fresh Fruit Freeze

Serves 4-6

2 cups very ripe fruit such as
 bananas, peaches, apricots,
 mangos, strawberries,
 blueberries, or raspberries
3/4 cup sugar
2 tsp. unflavored jello
2 T. water

2 T. fresh lemon juice
1 1/2 cups milk or pareve milk
2 egg whites, stiffly beaten
2–4 T. chopped nuts of any kind,
 optional
2 T. rum or cognac, optional

Puree fruits of your choice in blender, together with sugar. Soften
jello in water over flame to dissolve. Then add jello to fruit mixture
and blend some more. Pour in lemon juice and milk. Pour into a
9x13 inch tray, cover with foil and freeze about 4 hours, until
frozen at edges and still slightly soft in the middle. Rebeat at low
speed until smooth. Beat egg whites and fold in any of the optional ingredients. Refreeze. Remove from freezer 15–20 minutes
before serving for easier removal from pan.

Apple Compote

Serves 10-15

Suggestion:
This is great served
alone or with a
scoop of vanilla ice
cream on top of it.

20–35 apples, preferably tart
2–3 tsp. lemon juice
1 cup sugar

1 tsp. cinnamon
2 1/2–3 cups water

Peel and slice apples into a large pot. Toss with lemon juice. Add
remaining ingredients into pot and boil on a low flame until soft,
about 45 minutes to an hour. Can be pureed or left as is. Serve
chilled. Freezes well.

Surprise Apples

Serves 6

6 large apples, cored
handful of raisins, optional
1 cup orange juice

1/4 cup semi-dry white wine
cinnamon
brown sugar

Place cored apples into a small baking pan, fitting them together as firmly as possible. Use a smaller pan if necessary. Stuff the raisins into the empty core of each apple. Mix together the orange juice and wine and pour it over all the apples, including the holes in the center of the apples. Sprinkle brown sugar and cinnamon over the top. Bake covered for 45 minutes. Remove from oven. Serve warm or cold.

Fruit 'n Nut Relish

Serves 6

2–3 cups cranberries, rinsed
2 apples, peeled and diced
1 pear, peeled and diced
1 seedless orange, peeled and chopped
1 cup raisins
1/2–1 cup brown sugar

1 cup orange juice
1 1/2 tsp. cinnamon
1 cup walnuts, very coarsely chopped

Note:
If you don't use packaged products on Pesach, delete the jello and add 1/4 cup more of the red wine and a bit less water.

In large saucepan, combine everything except nuts. Bring to a boil, then reduce heat and simmer for 30 minutes, stirring frequently. Cool. Stir in walnuts and refrigerate overnight.

Fruit Shake

Serves 2–3

1/2 cup strawberries
1/2 cup blueberries
1 banana

2 cups milk
2 tsp. vanilla sugar

Blend everything well until frothy. Add 2 ice cubes and blend again. Serve immediately.

For a thicker shake, add 2 scoops of ice cream.

For a parve shake, omit the milk and replace it with a cup orange juice.

For a frozen yogurt, blend the fruits with 1/2 cup milk, 1 1/2 cups plain yogurt and 1/4–1/2 cup sugar. Drink as is or freeze in cups with popsicle sticks.

Cranberry Relish

1 package red jello
1 cup boiling water
1 can cranberry sauce
1 can whole berry cranberry sauce
1 cup coarsely chopped walnuts

2 cups unsweetened applesauce
1 can mandarin oranges or 1 whole
    orange, peeled and pitted
2 cups canned pineapple pieces,
    drained

Suggestion:
These two recipes
taste great served
with any meat dish.

Empty jello into a large bowl. Pour boiling water over it and mix to smooth out the lumps. Mash up both cranberry sauces a bit with a fork and add to the bowl. Add in applesauce and nuts. Process the orange and pineapple pieces in a food processor until chunky, and add to bowl. Mix by hand and refrigerate until serving.

Rhubarb Delight

2 1/4 lbs./1 kilo rhubarb
1–1.5 lbs./500 grams fresh
    strawberries

10 apples, preferably tart
2 cups sugar
1 cup water

Peel and slice apples thinly and place in pot. Cut rhubarb into medium sized chunks and add into pot. Add sugar and water. Cover pot and simmer until soft, about 45 minutes. Taste for sweetness. Slice strawberries. Place into pot on top of all, and cook for 10 more minutes. Turn off flame and let cool. Refrigerate until ready to serve.

FRESH FRUITY IDEAS

Pineapplesauce

Serves 8–10

Suggestion:
Garnish with sliced
fresh strawberries
before serving.

25 apples, preferably tart
juice of one lemon
1 can pineapple chunks, drained

1 cup sugar
1–2 tsp.cinnamon
2 cups water

Peel and slice apples into a large pot. Add water, sugar, and cinnamon. Boil gently until soft, about 30–60 minutes. Then blend pineapples until crushed but not completely smooth. Blend the apples as well, or for a chunkier sauce, just mash with a potato masher while still hot. Combine fruit and let cool. Refrigerate.

Fruited Cheese Mold

Serves 8

1 package lemon or lime jello
1 cup boiling water
1 cup pineapple tidbits, drained
1 cup reserved juice from the
    pineapples, chilled

1 cup nonfat cottage cheese
1 cup plain yogurt
1 T. lemon juice
1 tsp. vanilla or vanilla sugar
seasonal fresh fruits

In a large bowl, dissolve jello in boiling water. Add cold pineapple juice and 4 large ice cubes. Stir until it resembles the consistency of unbeaten egg whites. Discard any ice that still remains. With electric beater, beat at high until whipped. In another bowl combine cottage cheese, yogurt, lemon juice and vanilla. Blend in a blender until smooth. Combine the two mixtures and mix on low speed until just combined. Fold in pineapple tidbits. Pour into serving bowl or jello mold and chill until serving. Garnish with seasonal fresh fruits such as sliced strawberries and kiwi.

MEASUREMENTS
& EQUIVALENTS

Common Abbreviations:

Ounce = oz.
Pound = lb.
Teaspoon = tsp./ t.
Tablespoon = T.
Cup = c.
Pint = pt.
Quart = qt.
Gallon = gal.

Measurement Conversions:

These weight measurements are not exact, but have been rounded off to make your converting in the kitchen easier.

1/4 ounce = 7 grams
1/2 ounce = 15 grams
1 ounce = 30 grams
4 ounces = 1/4 pound = 115 grams
8 ounces = 1/2 pound = 225 grams
12 ounces = 3/4 pound = 350 grams
16 ounces = 1 pound = 450 grams
2 pounds = 900 grams
2 1/4 pounds = 1 kilogram
4 1/2 pounds = 2 kilograms

Grams x .035 = Ounces
Kilograms x 2.2 = Pounds

Linear Measurements:

0.394 Inch = 1 cm.
1 Inch = 2.54 cm.
Millimeters x .04 = Inches
Centimeters x .4 = Inches

Other Measurements:

1 Tablespoon fresh herbs = 1 teaspoon dried herbs
1 teaspoon = 1/3 Tablespoon
3 teaspoons = 1 Tablespoon = 1/2 fluid ounce
1 1/2 teaspoons = 1/2 Tablespoon
2 Tablespoons = 1/8 cup = 1 fluid ounce
4 Tablespoons = 1/4 cup = 2 fluid ounces
8 Tablespoons = 1/2 cup = 4 fluid ounces
12 Tablespoons = 3/4 cup = 6 fluid ounces
16 Tablespoons = 1 cup = 8 fluid ounces = 1/2 pint

1/3 cup = 5 Tablespoons + 1 teaspoon
3/8 cup = 1/4 cup + 2 Tablespoons
2/3 cup = 10 Tablespoons + 2 teaspoons
5/8 cup = 1/2 cup + 2 Tablespoons
7/8 cup = 3/4 cup + 2 Tablespoons
2 cups = 1 pint = 16 fluid ounces
1 quart = 2 pints = 4 cups = 32 fluid ounces
1 gallon = 4 quarts

Volume:

Milliliters x .03 = Fl. Ounces
Liters x 2.1 = Pints
Liters x 1.06 = Quarts
Liters x .26 = Gallons

Temperature:

Celsius x 9/5 + 32 = Fahrenheit

Oven Temperatures:

Very cool = 250–275°F / 130–140°C
Cool = 300°F / 150°C
Warm = 325°F / 170°C
Moderate = 350°F / 180°C
Moderately hot = 375–400°F / 190–200°C
Hot = 425°F / 220°C
Very hot = 450–475°F / 230–250°C

Index

Recipes
FOR
GLUTEN-FREE NOODLES

Leek 'n Spinach Noodle Kugel

Serves 4–6

1 medium sized leek
2 cups frozen spinach
1 large onion, diced
2 scallions, diced, optional

2 eggs or 3 egg whites
2 tsp. salt
1/2 tsp. pepper
2 T. olive oil
1 package (200 grams) Gefen Gluten-Free Wide Shaped Noodles

Prepare Gefen Gluten-Free Noodles, thin or flat lokshen shapes, by boiling in rapid water for ONLY FIVE MINUTES. Drain and rinse very well. Place in a large bowl. Add oil and spices and mix.

In a separate pan, sautee onions, leek, and scallions with oil until soft. Add spinach and saute 5 more minutes. Turn off flame and pour the vegetables into the noodle mixture. Mix and pour out into a lined small pan such as an 8x8 inch pan or smaller. Bake uncovered at 350°F /180°C for 45 minutes until light brown on top. Cuts easiest when cold; serve warm.

Spaghetti Sauce

Serves 6

1 onion, diced
3 cloves garlic, diced
1 large green pepper, diced
1 small can sliced mush-rooms, optional
1/2 cup sliced olives, optional
1/4 cup olive oil
4 cups tomato sauce (Or 1 1/2 cups tomato

paste and 1 cup water)
1 1/2 T. salt
1/2 tsp. pepper
1 tsp. oregano
1/2 tsp. dried parsley
1/2 tsp. basil
1 bay leaf
2 T. vinegar
2 packages (400 grams) Gefen Gluten-Free Noodles (wide shaped or macaroni)

Sautee onion, garlic, and pepper in olive oil until light brown. Add optional mushrooms and/or olive rings. Saute two more minutes. Add tomato sauce, seasonings and vinegar and let sauce simmer for an hour.

Boil up Gefen Gluten-Free Noodles in boiling water for only 9 minutes. Drain immediately and rinse well with cool water. To serve, place some noodles on a plate, and spoon the hot sauce over it. For a dairy version, sprinkle some grated cheese on top of the hot sauce immediately before serving.

For a meat version, saute 2 diced onions, 2 cloves of garlic and one small green pepper in a large pan with 2 T. olive oil. Add in 2.5 lbs./ 1 kilo ground red meat or a mixture of ground meat and ground turkey, and brown. Keep stirring this with a wooden spoon to break up the meat pieces and to ensure that it will be browned on all sides. Cover with lid and allow it to simmer for 20 minutes. Add the above sauce ingredients (before it cooks) and let it simmer together on the stovetop for 1 hour. Serve over hot, cooked Gefen Gluten-Free Noodles.

Pollack Foodservice & Medical

Complete Suppliers to the Healthcare Community

Arthur Pollack / C.E.O.

P.O. Box 10298
1615 Collamer Ave.
Cleveland, OH 44110

Office: (216) 851-9911
Fax: (216) 851-9939
email: arthurp@pollakdist.com

146